Allen

GHOST TOWNS
of the Old West

GHOST TOWNS
OF THE OLD WEST

Photographs by Lynn Radeka

Text by Gary Topping

MALLARD
PRESS

An imprint of BDD Promotional Book Company, Inc.,
666 Fifth Avenue, New York, New York, 10103

MALLARD PRESS

An imprint of BDD Promotional Book
Company, Inc., 666 Fifth Avenue, New
York, New York 10103

ISBN 0-7924-5655-6

AN M&M BOOK

Ghost Towns of the Old West was prepared and produced by M & M Books,
11 W. 19th Street, New York, New York
10011.

Project Director & Editor Gary Fishgall
Editorial Assistants Maxine Dormer,
Ben D'Amprisi, Jr.; *Copyediting* Bert N.
Zelman and Keith Walsh of Publishers
Workhop Inc.; *Proofreading* Judith Rud-
nicki.
Designer Binns and Lubin/Martin Lubin
Separations and Printing Regent Pub-
lishing Services Ltd.

Previous pages: Main Street, Gold Point,
Nevada.

These pages: Detail of a cart, Molson,
Washington.

Contents

Introduction

American history, to most of us, is a success story. With only occasional setbacks, we have proudly created a new political system, established a strong economic power, forged a mighty military machine, and become a dominant player in the international arena. Closer examination, though, reveals unsettling undercurrents that suggest a less optimistic picture. Southern history, for one thing, has many elements of frustration, failure, and defeat. The quagmire of Vietnam taught us an unforgettable lesson about the arrogance of power. And western ghost towns remind us that all dreams do not come true, and that even when they do, they often do not endure.

Nor, perhaps, do our dreams always show us at our best. Most ghost towns are ruined monuments to materialism. While their histories often reveal courage in the face of great economic or physical risk, ingenuity in the solution of daunting technological problems, and the humane commitment to community development and/or the advancement in civilization, they also reveal greed, violence, corruption, and oppression.

Why, then, are we Americans so fascinated with ghost towns? What penitential impulse leads us to seek out these reminders of our failures? Perhaps those faded dreams that burned in our ancestors' breasts are perpetually rekindled in ours, in spite of the ghostly warnings of empty windows, abandoned mineshafts, and crumbling walls. Or perhaps there is something more profound, perhaps the fact that all American history is recent history, makes us yearn for antiquity, for ivy-covered ruins. America, as Nathaniel Hawthorne observed, is "a country where there is no shadow, no antiquity, no mystery, no picturesque and gloomy wrong, nor anything but a commonplace prosperity, in broad and simple daylight." Do ghost towns provide those shadows, those antiquities, those mysteries we lack?

All of the towns in this book have two principal elements in common. One is that each lost its economic base and with it the population that came to it in search of something better. Some of these communities burned brightly for a brief period and then disappeared. Others passed through several incarnations, tapping a succession of economic resources, before the final failure set in. Many of these towns still have residents, but most of those are caretakers guarding the historical integrity of a decaying place, or stragglers eking out livings from old mine tailings (ore waste heaps), or from grazing livestock in streets once built for stagecoaches and automobiles.

The other element that all of these towns share is authenticity. Some, like Alta, Colorado, are in the ruined condition left to them by history, with fallen walls, sagging roofs, and empty windows. Others, like Bannack, Montana, exist in what is called a state of "arrested decay." In these cases, some efforts have been made to stabilize structures in danger of collapse, but otherwise little or no renovation or reconstruction has been attempted. Still others, like South Pass City, Wyoming, have been at least partly restored to their original condition. Whatever their current physical state,

these are all places in which the visitor can experience something historically genuine; none are mere tourist traps, where the main attractions are gift shops and phony gunfights on Main Street.

Ghost towns have a past, as you will discover by reading the histories that are recounted in this volume. But do they have a future as well? Lynn Radeka's haunting photographs suggest that the future of most authentic ghost towns is precarious at best. The two worst enemies are tourist promoters and vandals. None of the photographs in this book show the grotesqueness to which promoters will descend in quest of the dollar, but several exhibit the ravages of modern barbarians with no historical or aesthetic sense.

Fortunately, our society has also produced advocates for those places our pecuniary economy has forgotten and our violent instincts have ravaged. For example, private citizens like Mr. Benny Lucero of Cabezon, New Mexico, have taken it upon themselves to protect the remnants of the communities in which they were raised, or to which they were beckoned by the mysterious ghosts that haunt those empty rooms. Elsewhere, state parks divisions, the Bureau of Land Management, and the U.S. Forest Service have understood the intangible value of those abandoned communities and have appointed rangers or other caretakers to protect their integrity.

The author and photographer offer this book, then, in the twofold hope that the ghost towns presented here will provide not only delightful images of our past but will also challenge the reader to wrestle with some of the disturbing implications of that past and encourage the public to cherish and protect its fragile material remains.

(Opposite) **The Old Mail Station in Shakespeare, New Mexico. A room with sleeping quarters is partially visible in this photo.**

Rocky Mountain States

(*Above*) In the early 1880s, cabins like the one in the foreground, owned by Joe Sawyer, housed about 1,000 miners in the Ashcroft area.

(*Opposite*) A close-up of the town jail. Ashcroft was not known as one of the rowdier mining towns in the West, but the long, isolated winters led to occasional conflicts among the miners.

(*Previous pages*) An overview of Animas Forks, Colorado.

Referring to the color-strewn alpine meadows around Pearl Pass between Aspen and Ashcroft, Colorado, a Cornish miner called Cousin Jack exclaimed, "It's a bloody flower garden." Miners are not well known for their aesthetic judgments, but Cousin Jack was probably not the only one to enjoy the sight of nature's bounty during the arduous journey to mineshafts located above 13,000 feet in the western part of the state. It was not a sight to last, of course. Soon came winter, which at that elevation was long, cold, and lonely, with snowpacks almost 30 feet deep blocking access to civilized comforts at lower altitudes.

In spite of such rigors, the town of Ashcroft flourished intermittently for more than 30 years. Haughty Ashcrofters often referred to Aspen, 1,500 feet below, as "the low country" and only narrowly lost out to their rival community in their 1881 bid to capture the county seat of the newly created Pitkin County. During its heyday in the early 1880s, Ashcroft boasted a population of about 1,000. Along Castle and Main, the two principal streets, one could find four hotels, general stores and saloons, a jail, and the offices of a newspaper, the *Ashcroft Herald*.

Rich deposits of silver and lead had been known to exist in the vicinity of Ashcroft as early as 1869, but equally rich sources of supply at more accessible elevations kept miners away, as did the resistance of the Ute Indians on whose reservation much of the mining district fell. Finally, in the fall of 1879, a bold prospector named Thomas E. Ashcroft ventured into the area with a group of settlers and laid out a town called Highland near the confluence of Conundrum and Castle creeks. Only two of his hardy band chose to brave the ferocious winter, but in the spring most of the remaining settlers returned. They created another town near Highland, which they called Chloride, then Castle Forks, then Ashcroft. With the establishment of Aschcroft, Highland was abandoned.

The ore bodies around Ashcroft turned out to be rich but not extensive. The most prolific producer was the Tam o' Shanter, a mine located at the amazing elevation of 13,572 feet. It was discovered in 1880 by a prospector whose name has not survived. After demonstrating the richness of his strike to three Leadville entrepreneurs, Colonel Chapin, Jake Sands, and H. A. W. Tabor, he persuaded them to buy him out for $100,000. The price may have been too high. Although Tabor and his partners had another good producer, the Montezuma, which combined with the Tam o' Shanter brought the partners $20,000 a month, the mines were expensive to work and generally operated at a loss until they were finally abandoned in 1892. But losing $100,000 would not have bothered Tabor much. He was an extravagant

spender whose lavish home in Ashcroft is said to have featured gold-encrusted wallpaper and who supposedly spent $12 million in 13 years. Tabor was not the only colorful character in Ashcroft. Another was the saloon keeper, mayor, and weatherman Dan McArthur, who virtually ran the town from 1886 to 1920. His saloon was the community's social center, partly because it admitted women as well as men, and partly because McArthur owned a primitive cylinder phonograph and a substantial collection of records donated over the years by lowland vacationers. Curiously, McArthur also ran a weather bureau, which seems to have been a self-appointed job. Endowed—or cursed—with a driving compulsion to keep records, he took daily temperature

(*Above*) This stream, called Castle Creek, gave its name to one of Ashcroft's two main streets.

(*Opposite*) Ashcroft, Colorado, is located in a mountain valley at an elevation of about 13,000 feet. It is one of the highest mining communities in the West.

(*Right*) During its heyday, Ashcroft boasted a population of about 1,000. Along Castle and Main, the two principal streets, one could find four hotels, general stores and saloons, a jail, and the offices of a newspaper called the *Herald*.

(Right) Ashcroft has been reconstructed to appear much as it did in the 1800s, but some of the structures—there are fewer than a dozen in total—have been left in a state of ruin.

(Below) This photo, taken from the rear of the general store, shows clearly why the facades of such structures were called "false fronts." Ashcroft's isolation in the winter made the availability of food and other supplies at such outlets vitally important.

readings at 6:00 a.m., noon, and 6:00 p.m., and carefully recorded them. If the press of business kept him from his regular readings, he was said to have become very upset. He also devised a mysterious device for recording the depth of new snowfalls. It consisted of a block of wood 2 feet in diameter. Carefully positioning it to protect it from wind drifts, he developed an elaborate system that involved sweeping it at intervals and remeasuring it as it accumulated residues of snow. Although entrepreneurs like Tabor and his associates kept mines operational, Ashcroft's remoteness greatly diminished its general profitability.

Stage lines managed to approach the town from two directions, but the 12,000-foot mountain passes by which one reached Ashcroft itself were almost impossible for wagons to negotiate. The most practical way of getting there seemed to be by a "jack trail," a route for pack burros that began at a point called the "Transfer" which wagons could reach. Such transportation difficulties added greatly to the cost of working the none-too-dependable digs. Mines in the Aspen area produced more consistently, and when the Den-

This view from an Ashcroft hotel window suggests something of the place's scenic beauty. Although visitors could only reach the town by means of an almost impossibly difficult stage road, Ashcroft was nevertheless a popular vacation site.

Leadville entrepreneur H. A. W. Tabor owned interests in several Ashcroft mines. He was an extravagant spender whose lavish Ashcroft home was said to have featured gold-encrusted wallpaper.

During Ashcroft's heyday, the town had a bustling commercial district, of which this general store was a part. Today, the surrounding countryside is particularly scenic in the fall, when the many aspen trees begin to change color.

ver & Rio Grande Railroad reached that town in 1887, mining there became even more economical.

Thereafter, Ashcroft went into a steady decline. After the richest of its ores had been extracted, it began surrendering large numbers of residents to its old rival. By 1904, there were only about 100 diehards left.

But Ashcroft was not dead yet. After the local mines were sold to a New York mining syndicate in 1906, they began producing again, and the town enjoyed another decade of life, even though the lively days of old did not return.

During the first mining boom, Ashcroft fortune seekers had exploited the ore bodies rather sloppily. Spurred by the knowledge that rich ores lay in wait all around them, they had not wasted time on any but those of the highest grade. Consequently, the tailings, or the waste heaps from their diggings, still contained ores that could have been reworked profitably. But the syndicate miners chose to ignore those opportunities and instead reentered the mines that they considered hastily abandoned in the late 1880s.

The primary focus of their efforts was the Montezuma, which had deteriorated badly during 20 years of neglect. Water had seeped into the mine slowly even during its initial operational phase, although it had been ignored by the original miners. But during the years of inactivity, the seepage had formed an immense ice barrier near the mouth of the tunnel and a waist-deep lake further in. Carroll H. Coberly, a pick-and-shovel man for the syndicate, vividly remembered the odor of clothes drying each night around the stove in his tent after a day of chopping ice.

By the time of Ashcroft's second mining phase, roads had been laid which enabled wagons to reach town. Still, most of the supplies and ore were transported in and out on burros. The syndicate tried to reduce the bulk of its efforts by purchasing machinery for an ore reduction mill at the "Transfer," but

During the early 1880s, there were four hotels in Ashcroft, of which this was one.

before the plant could be completed the snow began to fall and it was left to rust during the winter. By the following spring, the syndicate had declared bankruptcy, even though it had a quarter of a million dollars in investment capital.

And still Ashcroft refused to die. The syndicate leased the mines to another entrepreneur, who hired mining engineer Bert Channing to try to make the operation viable. But the project seemed snakebitten. Channing died during the first winter of the new firm's ownership, and even after his successor got the mill finished and a tramway built to supply it with ore, snowslides destroyed several tram towers, as well as the boarding house and the blacksmith shop. Rebuilding was out of the question, and so mining in Ashcroft ceased. Enough of the old buildings exist today for the town to have been used once—for a television series—but the only regular economic activity comes from guided hunting trips provided by a nearby lodge.

17

(Above) About a dozen buildings remain in Animas Forks. Though the area is beautiful in the summer, snowfalls of up to 25 feet in the winter discourage permanent occupancy.

(Opposite) The Walsh house, whose living room bay window is shown here, is currently undergoing renovation. Forest rangers serve as caretakers at Animas Forks.

To anyone unacquainted with the Colorado Rockies, it seems incredible that a town located at an elevation of 11,000 feet could be surrounded by even taller mountains, but that is exactly the setting of Animas Forks, Colorado. Mineral Point, a neighbor 4 miles to the north, is even higher at 12,000 feet and it still looks up at several of Colorado's famous 13,000-foot peaks. Together, Animas Forks and Mineral Point make Denver, the state's famous mile-high capital, seem rather like a lowland city.

Living conditions in that "cold, arid, and intensely vertical world," as one Colorado historian has called it, are predictably harsh. During the early 1870s, when a silver rush brought the first miners into the San Juan Mountains of southwestern Colorado, snow depths of 25 feet were recorded at Animas Forks; the records are mercifully silent regarding temperatures. In a terrain that only grudgingly admits modern travelers with four-wheel-drive vehicles, early settlers found pack animals to be the only practical means of transport for men, machinery, and supplies.

Rich silver deposits were long known to exist in the San Juan Mountains, but it was not until 1871 that the Ute Indians, whose homeland included these ranges, were suffi-

ciently subdued by the U.S. army to allow significant prospecting. Once the quality of the ore became known, though, neither the forbidding terrain nor the hostile Indians were enough to keep miners out. Dozens of towns took root in several counties as fortune hunters ignored the adversities of climate and topography in their quest for wealth.

Animas Forks was established at the point where two tiny streams came together to create the Animas River. The quantity of water at that juncture was not great, but a downward decline in elevation more than compensated for the lack of natural resources. Indeed, water power was one of the main attractions of the site when the town was founded in 1875, because, as miners had already learned in other remote locations, it was often easier to import smelting machinery—a one-time chore—than to export many loads of ore. Once refined, however crudely,

the silver could be transported to market easily. So Animas Forks became an important ore reduction center for much of the mining district of the San Juan Mountains. By 1876, both the Dakota & San Juan Mining Company and the San Juan Smelting Company had constructed plants there and put them into operation.

These companies were successful, but the largest ore reduction plant in Animas Forks—indeed the largest in Colorado—was the Gold Prince mill, located 2 miles from town at the head of Mastodon Gulch. It was an amazing structure. Since the mill was partly owned by a steel company, its foundations, floors, and rafters were all supported by steel girders. In total, it was said that 400 carloads of structural steel went into the Gold Prince's construction. The mind boggles at the labor involved in transporting such a vast quantity of heavy cargo to the building site.

Beyond the material used in its con-

(Above) **The hip roof and siding on this miner's bungalow transcend the slapdash construction of many mining-camp residences, indicating something of the wealth of Animas Forks.**

(Opposite) **The San Juan Mountains' steep terrain may have challenged miners with avalanches and transportation problems during the 19th century, but it makes Animas Forks one of Colorado's most scenic ghost towns today.**

struction, the Gold Prince mill dwarfed all other mining structures in the San Juan district by virtue of its imposing size. At 336 feet by 184 feet on the exterior, it cost a half-million dollars, employed 150 men, and boasted a daily capacity of 500 tons of ore. The sound thundered down the valley as it pounded out the ore from the Gold Prince mine, which was connected to the mill by a 12,600-foot tramway that

20

(*Above*) The massive Gold Prince mill employed 150 men and boasted a daily capacity of 500 tons of ore. It was connected to the mine by a 12,600-foot tramway that cost $75,000 to build.

(*Right*) Most of the buildings in Animas Forks are of frame construction. The crude logs and dilapidated condition of this ruin suggest that it was built early in the town's development, before the area's mines began to pay handsomely.

cost $75,000 to build. Perhaps the modern reader, imagining this awe-inspiring operation, can forgive the hyperbole of a 19th-century spectator who maintained that "into insignificance sinks the boasted riches of the caves of Aladdin when compared with the vast wealth now blocked out in the Gold Prince mine."

With all of Animas Forks' wealth, community improvements became possible. Foremost among these was a better transportation system. Thus, pack trails were replaced in time by a narrow, steep road. During the 1890s, a little narrow gauge railroad of the type popular in so many Colorado mining areas reached Animas Forks. The terrain surrounding the town was so steep, however, that a separate rail bed did not seem economical, so the rails were placed right in the road. Eventually, as the community began to encounter hard times, the railroad was abandoned. Thereafter, the rails were torn out and the road restored.

Undoubtedly the most colorful resident of Animas Forks in its heyday was a Danish immigrant named Rasmus Hanson. Hanson was a flamboyant mining entrepreneur and speculator, typical of those who helped give the Gilded Age its name. Born in 1847, he was educated in Denmark in agricultural science, but when he arrived in Chicago at age 21 it was the stories of western mining bonanzas, rather than the prospects for agricultural achievement, that fired his imagination. He followed the lure of precious metals to Nevada, then Colorado, arriving in the San Juan distict in 1876. It seemed that everything he touched turned not to gold but to silver. Soon he had acquired several valuable mines including the Sunnyside, which was working the same vein as the Gold Prince. He then became one of the owners of the Gold Prince as well. In 1886 the town of Animas Forks elected him mayor.

Hanson's wealth and ostentatious lifestyle awed even the European aristocracy. On one trip to England, it was said that he offered to sell one of his mining properties for a quarter of a million dollars but met with reluctance on the part of prospective customers until the Prince of Wales endorsed the investment. In this instance, though, the royal support may not have been well founded, for after the turn of the century Hanson's luck began to waver. In 1904, he was even called home from a European honeymoon to face huge financial losses. Despite this crisis, Hanson was gradually able to extricate himself from financial difficulties and by the time he died in 1909 a good part of his wealth had been recovered.

Animas Forks, like many western silver mining towns, died during the severe economic depression that followed the Panic of 1893. The causes for the depression's impact on the West can be traced to the abundance of silver during the 1870s. This bounty led debt-ridden western and southern farmers to call for the expansion of U.S. currency based on an accelerated coinage of silver. Responding to this demand, the Treasury Department, through the Bland-Allison Act of 1878 and the Sherman Silver Purchase Act of 1890, agreed to purchase and coin specified minimum amounts of the precious ore. But a return to fiscal conservatism in response to the Panic of 1893 caused the government to repeal the Sherman Act, and the price of silver plummeted. Silver mines and mills all over Colorado and the other Rocky Mountain states closed down. Animas Forks was gradually abandoned. The spectacular mountain scenery has so far been insufficient, in the absence of solid economic reasons, to lure residents to brave the valley's ferocious climate and isolation. Today the once-booming community lies silent in its lofty solitude.

(Opposite) The modesty of this miner's residence suggests that it was a product of the pick-and-shovel days of the early 1870s, before heavy machinery and better transportation opened up the real wealth of the area.

(Right) Because of Animas Forks' extreme elevation, transporting ore from the local mines was extremely difficult. In this photo, a group of hardy souls are loading up their burros for the downward trek through the San Juan Mountains.

(Below) The San Juan Mountains as they appear today are visible in the background of this overview of Animas Forks' remains.

(Above) A 6-mile drive over a steep dirt road leads to Alta, Colorado, a former mining camp in the San Juan Mountains near Telluride, Colorado.

(Opposite) Most of Alta's structures show considerable decay inside. The town has no current residents and no preservation or restoration program. Most deterioration is from natural causes, not vandalism.

Today Telluride is a small resort town in the San Juan Mountains in the southwestern part of Colorado. Each year thousands of visitors attend the river-runner rendezvous, bluegrass music festivals, and other get-togethers in Telluride's alpine environment. Those few visitors who explore the history of the area learn that Telluride was once the hub of a network of silver and gold mines in the surrounding mountains, and the remains of ghost towns attest to the area's former prosperity. Alta, Colorado, a few miles southeast of Telluride, was one of the most prosperous of those communities. The Gold King mine, whose Black Hawk tunnel tapped into the rich St. Louis and Alta veins, produced an estimated $15–20 million worth of ore during the mine's operation, which lasted from the 1870s to 1945.

Mining in the San Juan Mountains is hampered by the fact that the hillsides are so steep the world seems to stand on edge, so that even getting to the richest deposits which lie at the highest elevations is a major problem. Getting the ore out is even more difficult. But the placer miners who found gold in the gravel of the San Miguel River near Telluride in the early 1870s were inexorably drawn upward

The Gold King mine produced an estimated $15–20 million worth of ore between the 1870s and 1945. The operation's mill, seen here, refined the gold at the site, thereby saving the Gold King's owners the expense of transporting the raw ore out of the mountains.

toward the source of the precious metal. Their quest led them from Telluride over Boomerang Hill to the discovery of the Gold King and Alta mines, where they built the community of Alta in 1878. Although the first 10 sacks of ore from the Gold King yielded $5,000 in gold, prosperity was not immediate because only burros could negotiate the steep terrain to remove the ore.

Alta's eventual prosperity was largely due to the genius of Lucien Lucius Nunn, a lawyer who arrived in Telluride in 1888. Nunn was an admirer of Napoleon, whom he somewhat resembled in his facial features and diminutive stature. He resembled Bonaparte in his ambition as well and in a few years had taken over the local bank and acquired extensive real estate and mining interests. Although Nunn knew nothing about electricity, he conceived the idea of constructing a hydroelectric power plant at Ames on the south fork of the San Miguel River about 2½ miles from Alta, where the river dropped some 500 feet in less than a mile. His purpose in fostering this venture was to use the power to run a large stamp mill at the Gold King mine. By refining the gold at the site, he could substantially reduce the expenses of transporting the ore out of the mountains.

Nunn convinced George Westinghouse that the Ames power plant would be a good place to test Westinghouse's idea of transmitting electrical power over a considerable distance by using high-voltage alternating current. On June 20, 1891, Nunn threw the switches that turned on the new power plant, and the Gold King mill began to run in what was the first application of electricity to mining technology. A peripheral advantage, though not a minor one to the miners and other residents of Alta, was that the power line made electric lights possible, both in the residences and in the mines.

Mining at Alta was big business and required a large work force, which in turn mandated the construction of multistory boarding houses like the one pictured here.

(Following pages) Although wages were low and working conditions poor, Alta's residents could enjoy spectacular views of the surrounding San Juan Mountains.

29

Electrical power was not the only technological advance for which Alta was famous. Also in 1891, the Rio Grande Southern Railroad reached Ophir, another mining town between Telluride and Alta. As the extent of the veins at Alta became known and the extraction of the ore increased, mine operators found even the efficient electric stamp mill too slow for their needs. Looking for a way to transport ore in large quantities to the railroad at Ophir, they decided to construct a spectacular aerial tramway down the mountainside. Parts of this marvel are still visible today. Thereafter the mill was only used to concentrate the ore crudely, for further refinement could take place at larger sites elsewhere.

For some reason, Alta was never incorporated as a town, though it was certainly eligible for incorporation. Although Altans had to journey to Ophir or Telluride for religious services, the community had a large white school and many private homes. Single miners lived in a three-story bunkhouse with an outside stairway, which is still standing.

Technological progress, economic prosperity, and urban development are not the whole story of Alta, Colorado, for the town, like its nearby sister communities, has a history of violence and labor strife. Angered at the immense riches being reaped by the mine owners and the pittance that they were earning for laboring long hours under often dangerous conditions deep in the earth, miners all over the Telluride district turned to militant labor organizers during the early years of the 20th century. In 1901, the Western Federation of Miners, which had organized most of the Telluride workers, called a strike to protest the oppressive contract system in the mines. The mine operators countered by bringing in nonunion men, or "scabs." Violence erupted, and the scabs were defeated. Two years later another strike was called when one of the mills began using nonunion laborers. This time the state militia under the leadership of Maj. Z. T. Hill was called in. Hill's methods were ruthless. He imposed martial law on the entire district, took over the telephone and telegraph lines, and rounded up more

than 80 union organizers whom he deported on the railroad after beating up some of their leaders. This time the union lost. On April 5, 1904, after almost three months of strife, the Telluride Mine Owners' Association reopened the mines in the district with nonunion labor.

The mines at Alta continued to produce, its three mills continued to process ore, and the community continued to prosper. Then in 1945, the last of the mills burned, the other two having already been destroyed by fire. There seemed little reason to rebuild, since the ores had been petering out for some time, and the community was soon abandoned. Alta today is an increasingly popular side trip for summer visitors to Telluride. It offers satisfaction to those with an interest in spectacular scenery as well as aficionados of mining history.

This boarding house played host to Alta's single miners. During the bitter mine strike of 1904, company owners succeeded in replacing its unionized occupants with nonunion workers.

In contrast to the large boarding house on the opposite page, which was occupied by single miners, modest miners' cabins, such as the one shown here, served as homes for entire families.

(Top) An admirer of Napoleon, whom he somewhat resembled, attorney Lucien Lucius Nunn was largely responsible for Alta's prosperity. Within a few years of his arrival in town, he had taken over the local bank and had acquired extensive real estate and mining interests.

(Above) In 1903, Maj. Z. T. Hill of the Colorado state militia ruthlessly quelled a miners' strike in Alta by imposing martial law on the entire district, taking over the telephone and telegraph lines, and running more than 80 union organizers out of town.

This old residence, with its imposing front stairs and porch, was probably home to a mine operator. The miners, who felt oppressed by their employers, severely resented the managers who lived in comfortable, substantial homes like this one.

The plenitude of timber in the San Juan
Mountains and the prosperity of the Gold
King and other mines at Alta made possible
the construction of some very substantial
buildings.

(Above) Located near the summit of the famous pass that crosses the Continental Divide, South Pass City featured a business district that wound half a mile along the town's main street in its heyday. It even included a jewelry store and a bowling alley.

(Opposite) Desperadoes like Mountain Jack Alvese contributed to South Pass City's need for a strong jail. This relic of primitive law enforcement is one of the town's unrestored buildings.

I s there another trail that reverberates through western American history quite like South Pass? It is the West in a microcosm: the Indians, the explorers, the trappers, the miners, and the emigrants all used this passage through the Rocky Mountains. In one of geography's great anomalies, it easily spans North America's mightiest range whose northern reaches were virtually impassable by wheeled vehicles until the Machine Age leveled all geography. From the moment of its first discovery in October 1812 by a party of John Jacob Astor's trappers returning from the Pacific coast, it has amazed travelers by the ease with which it is traversed: one hardly feels the gentle climb at all and certainly finds it hard to believe that something as imposing as the Continental Divide has actually been crossed.

Although the returning trappers discovered the pass, knowledge of its existence was quickly lost. The historically effective discovery of South Pass came in 1824 when a Crow Indian related its existence to a party of Gen. William H. Ashley's trappers, including Jedediah Smith, James Clyman, and Thomas Fitzpatrick. The trappers were quick to appreciate its significance, as was the celebrated explorer John C. Frémont, who crossed it in 1842. Resting at the summit of the nearby mountain now known as Woodrow Wilson Peak, Frémont noticed a bumblebee which had fluttered up from the east and had lit on the knee of one of his men. "It was a strange place," he wrote, "the icy rock and the highest peak of the Rocky Mountains, for a lover of warm sunshine and flowers; and we pleased ourselves with the idea that he was the first of his species to cross the mountain barrier—a solitary pioneer to foretell the advance of civilization."

In contrast to the bumblebees, the two-legged pioneers for whom Frémont was the "Pathfinder" were already coming. Their numbers swelled over the next decades to the hundreds of thousands, and South Pass became the great gateway through which the West was settled.

Some of those who used the pass discovered gold there. Only weeks after Frémont's meeting with the bumblebee, a mountain man observed yellow flakes in a creek where he was setting beaver traps. He showed a small sack of the ore to his partners but was killed by Indians before he could return to exploit his discovery. The South Pass gold remained hidden until 1855, when a party of disappointed forty-niners returning empty-handed from California gave the pass a try and came up with the elusive metal.

Even then, the extent of the riches to be had there was not realized until the 1860s, when off-duty soldiers appointed to guard the pass against Indians began to take advantage of the area's riches. Other soldiers and civilian gold seekers joined them, and on November 11, 1865, Wyoming's first mining district was established on the site of what became South Pass City.

In the beginning, South Pass City, like many western mining towns, was a pretty uncivilized place. Subject to the laws of Dakota Territory but with no effective means of enforcing those laws, South Pass City attracted rough characters with names such as Vinegar Zeriner and Mountain Jack Alvese. There was trouble from without, too—the pass fell within the territory of several Native American tribes who were

(*Opposite*) The ferocious climate, conflicts with Indians, and lawless inhabitants discouraged families from coming to South Pass City. But in time civilization arrived and a schoolhouse, seen here, was erected in 1910.

(*Above*) This blacksmith shop would have been a welcome sight to the pioneers who crossed South Pass in covered wagons during the 1840s and 1850s, but the tools pictured here would not have arrived until the 1860s, after the mining boom had begun.

(*Right*) In 1870, South Pass City had a population of 4,000 and an estimated $3 million in earnings from the community's 10 largest mines. Saloons like the one shown here were lively places amidst such prosperity.

determined to rid themselves of the golddiggers.

Despite the obstacles, civilization made its inroads, however slowly. In the fall of 1867, an ex-freighter named William Tweed brought his wife and young son to live in South Pass City, and their home became a gathering place for homesick miners hungry for a woman's cooking.

Other families followed. By 1868 log structures were joined by clapboard houses made of lumber from no fewer than two sawmills. The business district wound for a half mile along the main street. In addition to the predictable saloons, South Pass City boasted a diverse commercial life, including a bowling alley and a jewelry store. There were four law firms to handle the inevitable conflicting mining claims and other disputes of the expanding community, while two doctors, uncertain about where their best financial prospects lay, divided their time between sickbeds and creek beds.

While the Carissa, the Carter, and several other rich veins of gold brought wealth, population, and fame to South Pass City, the town's most enduring contribution to western history was in the political arena. During the so-called Progressive Era around the turn of the century, western cities and states often took the lead in political reform, perhaps in part because frontier life fostered pragmatism over tradition. When

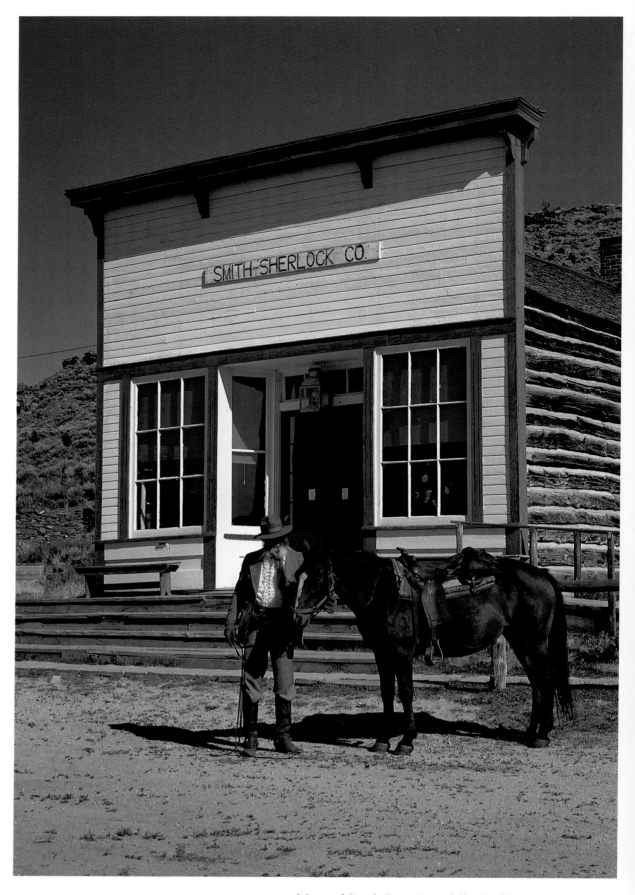

Thanks largely to the efforts of Esther McQuigg Morris, Wyoming became the first place in the United States where women could vote. Morris was subsequently appointed justice of the peace for South Pass City, the first woman in American history to hold such a post.

Many of South Pass City's fallen buildings have been reconstructed on their original sites. Log structures like the Smith-Sherlock store seen here replicate some of the town's earliest enterprises.

(Above) Meticulously reconstructed interiors, like the Carissa Saloon, seen here, re-create the lively atmosphere of South Pass City's commercial district during the 1860s and 1870s.

(Right) The reconstructed Sherlock Hotel lobby, rich in Victorian atmosphere, closely follows the design of the original structure built in the 1860s.

(Below) Among the first families to settle in South Pass City were the Tweeds, who arrived in the fall of 1867. William Tweed, an ex-freighter, and his wife made their home a gathering place for homesick miners hungry for a woman's cooking.

Wyoming became a territory in 1869, it quickly proceeded to give the rest of the country some political lessons, and thanks to Esther Morris, South Pass City was where the process began.

Esther McQuigg Morris, who took up residence in South Pass City during the formation of the new territorial government, determined to play a role in shaping Wyoming's political system. Orphaned at 11, she made her own way in the world, becoming a successful businesswoman. When her husband died, she was subjected to what she regarded as unjust property laws and as a consequence dedicated herself to the improvement of women's rights. During the campaign for the election of delegates to the territorial legislature, Mrs. Morris invited the two local candidates to a tea party and extracted from both a promise of support for women's right to vote.

William Bright, the victor, was as good as his word. Though an intense debate arose in the legislature over the bill Bright introduced, its proponents prevailed, and on December 10, 1869, Governor John A. Campbell signed it into law, making Wyoming Territory the first place in the United States where women could vote. The way was now paved for the political appointment of Mrs. Morris, who became justice of the peace for South Pass City. She was the first woman in American history to hold such a post.

In 1870, South Pass City had a population of 4,000 prosperous people and an estimated $3 million fewer in earn-

The large Carissa mine hugs a hillside in South Pass City. Its rich gold veins were among the most profitable in the district.

The interior of the Duncan mine. During South Pass City's heyday, 10 mines like this one were in operation. They produced an estimated $3 million worth of ore in less than a decade.

ings from the community's 10 largest mines. But, as the gold began to dwindle, the city declined as quickly as it had risen. In 1873, the county seat was moved to Green River, and the population of South Pass City was gradually reduced to almost nothing. Without the rich gold veins, and lacking convenient access to the railroad, the community could offer little to its inhabitants beyond isolation and fierce winter storms.

(Above) Piedmont is an abandoned railroad, lumber, and cattle town on the high plains of Wyoming, some distance from the modern railroad line and freeway.

(Opposite) The dilapidated roof of the Thinnes home shows the state of decay that has befallen most of the Piedmont structures. Fewer than a dozen buildings still stand here; some have even collapsed in recent years when preservation efforts have arrested the decay of other ghost towns.

I f a ghost town is simply a community that has lost its economic base, then Piedmont, Wyoming, is a mystery. Most 19th-century towns that eventually shut down were centered in their heyday on a single industry—often mining—to which other economic activity, such as mercantile operations and professional services, were subordinate. When the mines gave out, so did everything else. But Piedmont enjoyed a remarkably broad economic base: it was a station on the stagecoach line, a station on the Union Pacific Railroad, a lumber town, a charcoal manufacturing town, and a supply center for cattle ranchers and sheepherders. Yet no one today lives in Piedmont, and the only reminders of its once-thriving economy are some run-down buildings and several conical charcoal kilns. What killed Piedmont?

Although the Union Pacific Railroad was to give the town its greatest prosperity, the first settlers in Piedmont preceded the railroad by more than a decade. The family of Moses Byrnes moved there in 1857; it was joined by the Charles Guild family in 1864. The tiny community was in fact first called Byrnes, after its founding father, but confusion set in later when the railroad established a neighbor-

(Above) Railroad ties cut in the nearby Uinta Mountains were also used to build Piedmont residences such as the Thomas Byrnes home seen here.

(Opposite) This bare interior is all that remains of the Thinnes home. Although some of the structures in Piedmont have been fenced, none have been restored or otherwise protected.

ing community called Bryan, and Moses Byrnes graciously allowed the name to be changed to something more distinctive. Piedmont was selected as a means of alleviating the homesickness of Mrs. Byrnes and Mrs. Guild, who were sisters from the Piedmont area of Italy.

In its early years, Piedmont was a station on the overland stage line. Frontier depots were often lonely establishments, usually run by a single man or a single family who stabled fresh horses and prepared meals for passengers while they tried to guard against the Indian attacks to which they were highly vulnerable. Despite the bountiful timber supply in the Uinta Mountains just to the south of

the town, the station at Piedmont was a stone fortress with tiny porthole windows behind which the stationmaster could defend himself.

During construction of the transcontinental railroad in the 1860s, Piedmont enjoyed its first and greatest prosperity. The heavily timbered slopes of the Uinta Mountains along the Wyoming–Utah border—the only major mountain range in the United States with an east–west orientation— provided a welcome source of ties for the workers who were laying tracks along a line that paralleled the mountains to the north. The Coe & Carter Tie Company, which established a camp on the Black's Fork River at the foot of the mountains, used Piedmont as a source of supplies and for weekend entertainment.

Piedmont actually enjoyed two lives as a tie camp headquarters. Despite the $48,000 federal subsidy the Union Pacific Railroad received for construction through the mountainous terrain, the company used the cheapest and lightest materials it could find at a fraction of the anticipated cost and pocketed the remainder of the allocation. Thus the entire line had to be rebuilt before the end of the century. In 1896, an article in the local newspaper in Evanston, Wyoming, reported that Piedmont was enjoying an economic resurgence thanks to the laying of new track in the Uinta Mountains area.

Timber from the Uinta Mountains had other uses as well. Winters in the unprotected stretches of southwestern Wyoming are famous for their severity. Railroaders learned early that trains could be stopped for days by immense snowdrifts across the tracks, so long snowsheds resembling covered bridges were built of local timber to protect the line through the most vulnerable areas. Old-timers remember the carpentry of those snowsheds as being quite impressive, for the ferocious Wyoming winds could drive amazing quantities of powdery snow through even tiny chinks. The length and tight construction of the sheds gave uninitiated passengers the feeling of passing through tunnels, and in time actual tunnels did, in fact, replace the open-air structures. At the

same time, they eliminated the steep grade of Aspen Hill to the west of Piedmont. This construction too made use of local timber. It helped shore up the roofs of the passageways and provided ties for the new rails.

Even these construction efforts didn't exhaust the uses for Uinta Mountain timber. In the 1870s, as silver mining began to boom in the Wasatch Mountains east of Salt Lake City, shrewd Piedmont entrepreneurs recognized a potential market for charcoal to fuel the Utah silver smelters. Accordingly, they built five large kilns at a cost of $1,000 apiece to reduce wood to charcoal. Four of them remain today; the fifth was dismantled and the stone used to build a dam. They are impressive structures, 30 feet in diameter and 30 feet high, with 7-foot doorways. Although they were capable of large-scale production, coke from coal mines in Carbon County, Utah, eventually replaced Wyoming charcoal in

On August 10, 1896, Butch Cassidy registered at the Piedmont Hotel. It is believed that while he and a member of his gang were in town they planned the bank robbery that they committed three days later in Idaho.

the smelters, and Piedmont lost a primary industry.

Before the construction of the Aspen Hill tunnel, Piedmont was a vitally important stop on the railroad. Trains would pause there to pick up support engines. Known as "helpers," these engines provided the extra power needed for a train to climb eight steep and winding miles to the summit of Aspen Hill. A roundhouse—actually a triangular structure—was built in Piedmont to shelter those engines.

If the railroad brought prosperity to Piedmont, it also brought notoriety. At about 7:00 a.m. on August 10, 1896, the renowned train robber Butch Cassidy and a partner, probably one of his gang members named Bob Meeks, rode into town and registered at the Piedmont Hotel. Later that morning, the westbound train brought to town Robert Preston, an attorney from Rock Springs, Wyoming. Preston met with Cassidy and Meeks at the hotel while the train took on fuel, water, and extra engines. When the train left with Preston again on board, Cassidy and Meeks rode away to the north. Lawmen believed that the Wild Bunch's subsequent robbery of the bank in Montpelier, Idaho, on August 13 was planned during that brief meeting.

After the turn of the century, the railroad completely realigned its route through southwestern Wyoming, and Piedmont was left isolated at the foot of the mountains that had brought the community its greatest prosperity. Forced to rely, as at the beginning of its history, on wandering stockmen for its livelihood, Piedmont learned quickly that it could not compete with the burgeoning nearby community of Evanston. The town died a lingering but inevitable death as the population of 200 during the railroad days dropped to 35, then, by the 1940s, to nothing. The visitor today is greeted by little but a few dilapidated buildings and the empty stare of the tiny smokeholes in the remaining charcoal kilns, as their Cyclops eyes contemplate the barren Wyoming landscape.

The Piedmont graveyard offers a commanding view of the community that had been a frontier stage depot and later an important railroad stop.

Although they resemble tombs from some ancient civilization, these kilns were used to turn Uinta Mountain timber into charcoal for Utah silver smelters.

The Northwest

(Above) Located high in the Montana mountains, Garnet is approached by a steep dirt road that can be treacherous in wet weather.

(Opposite) The simple poetry of this still life at the J. K. Wells Hotel is deceptive. At left is a kerosene lamp which, along with the crude chimneys of the town's structures, created a serious fire hazard. Indeed, Garnet was destroyed by fire in 1911.

(Previous pages) Buildings on Morning Star Street, Silver City, Idaho.

According to the poet, "While the world is filled with sorrow/ And men must fume and fret/ It is day all day in the daytime/ And there's no night in Gar-a-net." Walt Whitman obviously had no reason to worry about competition from this anonymous scribe who often sang the praises of Garnet, Montana, in the town's local newspaper. But the poet's exuberance expressed a well-founded optimism. The gold strikes along Bear Creek in the Garnet Range were the last of Montana's rich deposits, and they paid out democratically. While most gold and silver mines yielded high profits to the primitive technology of the pick and the pan only briefly before expensive machinery became necessary to plumb their depths, the Garnet mines were a "poor man's bonanza" and remained a haven for placer mining right to the end.

Mining started in the Garnet Range in the fall of 1865, when surface deposits along Bear Creek and its tributaries attracted men like Col. G. W. Morse, who were working other Montana mines. Soon it became apparent that the range's real value lay many feet below the creek beds. Here, in deeper placers along the bedrock, the weight of the gold had caused the precious ore to sink through looser and

lighter layers of material over time. Colonel Morse, in fact, found a nugget weighing 32 ounces in one such claim.

But the Garnet placers yielded up their riches slowly, and, unlike other new finds, this one inspired no headlong rush of eager fortune seekers. Finding the placers was easy—they were concentrated in a 15-foot-wide band directly beneath the creeks—but getting the gold out was another matter. With the creek directly overhead, keeping water out of the mineshafts created major problems. Most miners labored in pairs. As one operated a hand windlass on the surface, the other sent up alternating buckets of water and ore. It was said that such condi-

tions, working in knee-deep water far below the surface in near darkness, created a type of man known as a "Beartown tough," named for the town where most of the miners lived. The Beartown tough looked something like a bear, holding his head low, his feet far apart, and squinting against the muddy water dripping from the walls and ceiling of his tunnel.

The community of Beartown and the waterlogged toughs who populated it had seen their best days by 1868. After that, some mining continued in the area, but real prosperity awaited the realization, some 30 years later, that the Garnet Range's true wealth lay in gold-bearing quartz deposits found in the mountains themselves. One entrepreneur, Bror A. C. Stone, demonstrated the profitability of quartz

mining in 1886 when he erected a small stamp mill and extracted $10,000 from a quartz vein.

In 1896, a group of Chicago investors purchased another claim, called the Mammoth, and built a bigger stamp mill to reduce the mine's quartz ore. It was profitable enough to encourage yet another group of miners—those at Samuel I. Richey's Nancy Hanks claim—to dig a little deeper, and they struck the Garnet Range's

(Top) Col. George W. Morse was among the Montana miners attracted to the Garnet Range in the 1860s. Perhaps his greatest claim to fame was the 32-ounce nugget that he once found in a deep placer along the bedrock of Bear Creek.

(Above) John D. Brown—better known as "Whiskey" Brown—ran a short-order emporium in Garnet during the town's heyday. It was open 24 hours a day.

The garments hanging on nails in this old cabin typify the kind of rugged apparel that miners wore to work. The Garnet Range contained rich deposits of both gold and silver, but it took long days of hard labor to work them profitably.

best vein. Nancy Hanks ore assayed at $250 per ton in gold, and $25 in silver.

The long-delayed gold rush finally came to the area, and the town of Garnet sprang up. Hampered by the hellishly tight bends on the road called the "Chinee Grade," which came up from Beartown, Garnet residents found it uneconomical to import high-grade building materials. Instead, they fashioned their town from those items that the mountains themselves provided: logs chinked with mud from the creek, rough-hewn lumber in very limited quantities, and clay for fireplaces.

The fireplaces turned out to be a costly mistake. In time, the clay cracked from the heat of the big fires that Montana winters required and buildings burst into flame. In fact, much of the town burned in 1911. Garnet never got electricity, and the coal oil lamps that were used for illumination created additional fire hazards, as did the acetylene used to light the Garnet Hotel.

Despite the hazards, Garnet thrived. Predictably, the most successful businesses were the town's four saloons, but two large hotels, the Garnet and the Wells, offered surprisingly sumptuous accommodations and cuisine. Garnet even boasted what may have been Montana's first fast-food outlet, J. D. Brown's short-order emporium, which was open 24 hours a day.

Social life in Garnet was impressive in its diversity. One saloon, the Bella Union, featured an orchestra that played nightly. For special occasions, more elaborate entertainments were available. On New Year's Eve, 1899, Garnet residents enjoyed a gala costume ball in nearby Coloma, Montana. The following year, the locals outdid

(*Above*) Although water pipes are visible on the exterior of the J. K. Wells Hotel, the town never got electricity. The hotel was illuminated by acetylene lamps.

(*Opposite*) Unlike many mines that required expensive technology to yield their riches, those at Garnet's paid off democratically. Even some of the prospectors who used ore buckets like the one pictured here got lucky.

(*Left*) This comfortable chair in Kelly's Saloon—one of four such establishments in Garnet—indicates something of the good accommodations available in the town, despite its rough appearance.

(*Below*) Miners of the Nancy Hanks claim, seen here, located the richest vein in the Garnet Range. Nancy Hanks ore assayed at $250 per ton in gold, and $25 in silver.

(Above) Although it was not ornate, the J. K. Wells Hotel, seen here in close-up, offered travelers comfortable rooms and a surprisingly elaborate cuisine

(Opposite) As the advertisements fronting the bar suggest, smokers and chewers alike were welcome at Kelly's Saloon.

their rivals by staging a "Grande Masquerade" ball with an orchestra consisting of a local violinist and pianist and a cornet player imported from faraway Missoula. After the midnight unmasking, the Wells Hotel served a banquet for the 56 revelers. These and other balls often began at 9:00 in the evening and ended at 4:00 the following morning.

The Garnet school was an austere structure obviously devoted purely to intellectual endeavor, for it had no windows to tempt the wandering gaze of daydreaming scholars. After some of the older students were noticed hanging around the faro and blackjack tables in the saloons during the summer when school was closed, a three-month summer session was added. The school even prompted a commendation from that celebrated but anonymous Garnet poet: "There's a school up here in Garnet/ That is tough/ The pupils are bright as dollars/ But they're rough."

During its heyday in the late 1890s, Garnet could claim a population of almost 1,000, but the Klondike gold rush and the diminishing returns of the quartz mines began draining people away. As one historian put it, for a time it seemed that Garnet was going downhill in every direction. The 1911 fire was a tragic blow to the community, and even though the mines enjoyed a brief resurgence during the 1930s, Garnet's best years were over.

The relative youth of Garnet no doubt helps account for the remarkably good condition of the town today. Some 50 buildings remain, administered by the Bureau of Land Management as one of Montana's best-preserved ghost towns.

(Above) Preserved as a state park, Bannack includes several dozen buildings along a lengthy main street.

(Opposite) The interior of the Masonic Hall. Although the outlaw Henry Plummer brought Bannack its greatest notoriety, much of the town's citizenry was law-abiding and its social and cultural life impressive.

Nestled at the foot of the Bitterroot Range is the town of Bannack, located in the southwestern region of Montana near the Idaho border. The town's importance in Montana's early territorial period was immense. It was there that the state's first major gold strike was made, and it was there that the first capital of the territory was situated. It was there too that Henry Plummer made his home. Plummer was a notorious robber and killer whose career in some ways eclipses even that of his more famous New Mexico counterpart, Billy the Kid.

It was overcrowding among Idaho fortune seekers that first led to the discovery of gold at Bannack. That took place in 1862, when a party of prospectors bound for Idaho heard that all the best locations had already been taken and switched their destination to the Deer Lodge Valley of present-day Montana. Two members of the party, John White and William Eads, were panning in Willard's (now Grasshopper) Creek on July 28 when they discovered substantial quantities of gold. Their primitive technology hardly revealed the richness of their strike, but it was enough to draw hundreds of other miners to the area, along with the usual contingent of gamblers and suppliers from as far away as California and Nevada.

The town in the arid sagebrush gulch grew explosively. By the end of the year, it had a population of 500, and double that in 1863. A line of tents on both sides of a main street gave way quickly to log, frame, and even brick structures.

In September 1863, at the height of Bannack's prosperity, Sidney Edgerton, chief justice of Idaho Territory, was held over in Bannack by severe winter weather. He was so impressed by the new town and its economic prospects that, when he returned home, he began a campaign to get Congress to create the new Territory of Montana. Congress acted on his advice on May 26, 1864, and Edgerton, whose campaign had evidently not been devoid of personal ambition, became the new territory's first governor. Edgerton's support was probably behind the selection of Bannack as the temporary capital of the new territory. That proved to be only a brief, shining moment for the new town, as the first Montana legislature met there only once (in Bannack's new brick hotel) and then decided to convene in nearby Virginia City, whose lucrative mines and population of 10,000 had outstripped the older town.

Although Bannack's glory seemed to have vanished as quickly as it had appeared, the town was not finished yet. In 1866, a group of local citizens decided that the gold-hungry nomads who had fled to Virginia City had given up on their town too easily. The problem, they thought, was not a lack of gold but an insufficiency of means by which to extract it. To rectify the situation, they dug an extensive system of

(*Top*) In spring 1895, mining entrepreneur Fielding L. Graves introduced an electric dredge into the Bannack area to work the creek bottoms. His success gave a lucrative burst of life to the town's dwindling fortunes.

(*Above*) Sidney Edgerton, chief justice of the Idaho Territory, campaigned vigorously for the creation of a Territory of Montana. On May 26, 1864, Congress acted on his advice, after which Edgerton became the new territory's first governor.

The lobby of the Meade Hotel. After Bannack
was designated the capital of the Territory of
Montana, the first session of the newly formed
legislature was held in this establishment.
Then the legislators adjourned to the more
prosperous Virginia City.

ditches which brought creek water to remote areas where gold placers of known richness existed. In all, three ditches were created, the longest of which was 44 miles; all of them were dug with picks and shovels.

The initiative of the town's boosters indeed revived Bannack's prosperity, but eventually even the ditch-fed sluiceboxes stopped producing precious metals. Then, in the spring of 1895, a mining entrepreneur named Fielding L. Graves decided another technological advance was worth the risk, and he brought in an electric dredge to work the creek bottoms. Two successive weekly runs produced $22,000 and $38,000—surely enough to excite even the most conservative speculator. Graves' idea caught on, and during the next two years a total of five dredges were put to work in the area, though the fifth capsized while it was being installed.

Placer mining dominated the Bannack digs, but other methods of extraction were used as well. As early as 1862 a stamp mill was brought in to crush gold-bearing quartz deposits. It was a water-powered device, but in 1864 a larger, steam-powered mill was installed at a cost of $25,000. Finally, in 1914, a cyanide mill was briefly tried in the quartz deposits.

In the meantime, the immense wealth of southwestern Montana had attracted a host of miners to the area. Some were honest, hardworking folk like those who dug the three great ditches, but Bannack also had its share of those seeking a shortcut to prosperity. Which brings us back to the infamous Henry W. Plummer, who arrived in Montana in 1862 having already

(Above) The Meade Hotel in the rear of this photo is an impressive brick structure. It was built in the early 1860s, during the town's first gold rush.

(Opposite) More than a few of the graves at Bannack were filled by the notorious outlaw Henry Plummer, who used his post as sheriff to mask his true professions—robber and murderer.

forged a long record of robberies and murders in the mining districts of California, Washington, and Idaho.

Plummer's great asset was the fact that he looked so clean-cut. Young, handsome, and impressive in his bearing, he was a born con man. Typically, he would arrive in a new town and masquerade as an honest citizen while covertly leading a gang of robbers. Shortly after settling in Bannack, Plummer, who was still in his twenties, shot Jack Cleveland, a former partner in crime. Not only was he acquitted of the murder, he was even elected sheriff by the citizens of Bannack. After that, Plummer had the perfect cover for a career in crime. While pretending to protect successful miners and their gold shipments from outlaws, he used the information to which his job gave him access to make his gang extraordinarily successful. Thanks to Henry, more than 100 victims were robbed or murdered before he was found out.

Just as in the countless western movies for which Plummer's career served as an inspiration, he and his gang were ultimately defeated by a vigilante committee of citizens from Bannack and Virginia City. Indeed, a remarkable period of vigilante justice ran its turbulent course before law and order once again reigned in Montana. Plummer himself met his end on the Bannack gallows on January 10, 1864. He was not yet 30 years old.

Located at the foot of the Bitterroot Range in southwestern Montana, Bannack was the site of the state's first major gold strike and the first capital of the Montana territory.

(*Right*) During the 1890s, a host of Bannack citizens gathered in front of the hotel to have their picture taken. Among those identified by number are the hotel manager, Mrs. Cora Jackson (2, on the balcony), Ed Smith Bale, one of the vigilante department's sheriffs (3, ground floor center), and Smith's wife (1, on the balcony).

(*Below*) With the exception of the Meade Hotel, most of the buildings in Bannack are of frame construction or, like this old residence, of logs chinked with clay.

In 1866, three long ditches were built in Bannack to bring water to sluice boxes like the one at right here. Still, in the long run, more advanced technology proved necessary to extract Bannack's elusive gold.

Most of the buildings in Bannack are open, but few contain historic exhibits or artifacts like this barber chair in Skinner's Saloon.

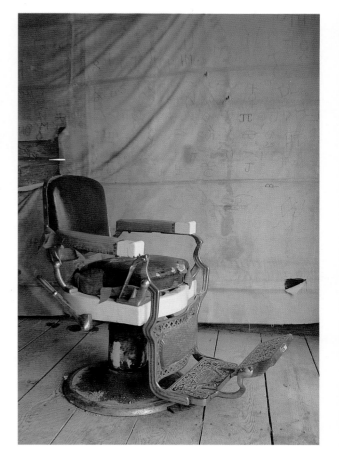

(Above) At its height, Silver City had a population of about 3,000. Its diversified economy featured specialized businesses like the meat market at right in this photo.

(Opposite) This is the front entrance of Silver City's Independent Order of Odd Fellows Hall. Fraternal, religious, and civic organizations flourished in many western mining towns alongside saloons and other rowdy establishments.

Known as the queen of Idaho ghost towns because of its size and state of preservation, Silver City offers compelling historical reasons for a visit: the richest vein of silver in the United States was discovered here, one of the most serious mining wars was fought here, and the city boasted one of the most colorful newspapers in the West. But even those who have a tin ear for history and literature can find Silver City worth a look-see. The spectacular view from the summit of 8,051-foot War Eagle Mountain is worth the trip all by itself. On a clear day one can see, if not quite forever, then perhaps into more states than from any other vantage point in the country. With a telescope, one can view the Tetons in Wyoming, a bit of Montana, the Wasatch Mountains in northern Utah, a butte in Washington, and substantial portions of Nevada, Oregon, California, and of course Idaho.

If the miners who founded Silver City in 1864 appreciated the view, none recorded the fact. It was not that they didn't see it, for they were all over War Eagle Mountain, but the far horizon and its aesthetic delights were not their concern. Their eyes were on the ground where the mountain's rich gold and silver veins were located.

Although Silver City boasts some very impressive buildings, most miners lived in more modest dwellings like this residence near Washington Street.

Silver City's colorful history began in 1863, when a prospector named Michael Jordan led 29 of his colleagues from the Boise area down into southwestern Idaho in search of the mythical Lost Blue Bucket mine. That legendary strike eluded them, but what they found must have been better than any tall tale. Their first samples of gold and silver suggested that they had discovered a vein even richer than the famous Comstock Lode of Nevada. Altogether three successive towns played host to the flood of miners in the area. Boonville was the first, but it was located between two steep mountains. It had no room to grow. Ruby City came next, but it was poorly planned. Worse, it couldn't accommodate expansion either. There were even those who said it had been laid out by a blind cow. Finally, in 1864, Silver City was constructed a mile south of Ruby City. Its first structures consisted of whatever could be dragged down from the neighboring town.

Silver City grew rapidly during the great rush of miners. In 1866 Silas Skinner completed a toll road into the new community, thereby proving that digging for ore was not the only way to make money in southwestern Idaho. Shortly thereafter, the local newspaper, the *Owyhee Avalanche*, established a telegraph line to Winnemucca, Nevada, so that Silver City residents could keep abreast of world events.

The urban scale of Silver City was, and is, quite impressive. The Idaho Hotel was an imposing frame building with 50 rooms; local promoters claimed that it was as large as any hotel in the territory. The elegant old structure is showing a few wrinkles and sags today, but it remains in business. In 1866, Silver City became the seat of Owyhee County. By the following year, the population had grown to perhaps 3,000 and no less than two schools—one in the schoolhouse and the other in the assay office—were in session. Catholics met on Sundays in a fine church they purchased from some Episcopalians, while the Protestants had to be content

In 1866, Silver City became the seat of Owyhee County. The archways of the courthouse are still standing, next to which are the remains of the town drugstore.

(Top) Currently under renovation, Stoddard House exemplifies the elegance of Silver City's best buildings.

(Above) A fine parade was staged in Silver City on Independence Day, 1866, the year that the town became the seat of Owyhee County. According to the local newspaper, the procession included "young ladies representing the States and Territories and children of the schools with flags."

(Opposite) Silver City, Idaho, is often called the "queen of ghost towns." Nestled high in the mountains, it is being preserved and renovated by a handful of dedicated residents.

with services held in Jones Hall, the Orofino Saloon, and the Masonic Hall.

Two major conflicts over mining claims lent a sanguine note to Silver City history. The area's prospectors had established placers, that is, surface claims worked with pans and rockers, but wiser heads later determined that the real riches lay in underground veins. Then some prospectors near the Hays and Ray claim discovered a very rich vein adjacent to their own. Since mining law held that continuous veins were part of the same claim, they worked their discovery fiercely, anticipating a challenge to their claim by Hays and Ray. The challenge soon came, but in the meantime, the Poorman—as the new claim was called— had produced a half-million dollars in gold and silver ore, assayed at 80 percent. And that had come from a ledge only 18 inches wide worked over a six-day period. A judge eventually effected a compromise between the two claims, and over the next six months the vein produced an even million dollars.

The other major dispute was resolved in a less peaceful manner. It too arose over conflicting claims, this time between the Ida Elmore and the Golden Chariot mines. When miners from the latter broke into the Ida Elmore shaft and at gunpoint forced their opponents into an underground retreat, a shooting war—known as the "Owyhee County War"—erupted. It continued for three more days and resulted in the death of mine owner J. Marion More. News of the conflict reached all the way to the governor's mansion, leading the territory's chief executive, D. W. Ballard, to dispatch emissaries to Silver City and to force the miners to negotiate. When diplomatic initiatives failed, Ballard ordered

(Right) Silver City Catholics bought the church shown here from the Episcopalians, but other denominations in town had no houses of worship. They had to hold services wherever they could.

(Below) The parlor of the Idaho Hotel is the very picture of Victorian clutter. This venerable structure, once promoted as being as large as any hostelry in the territory, is still open for business.

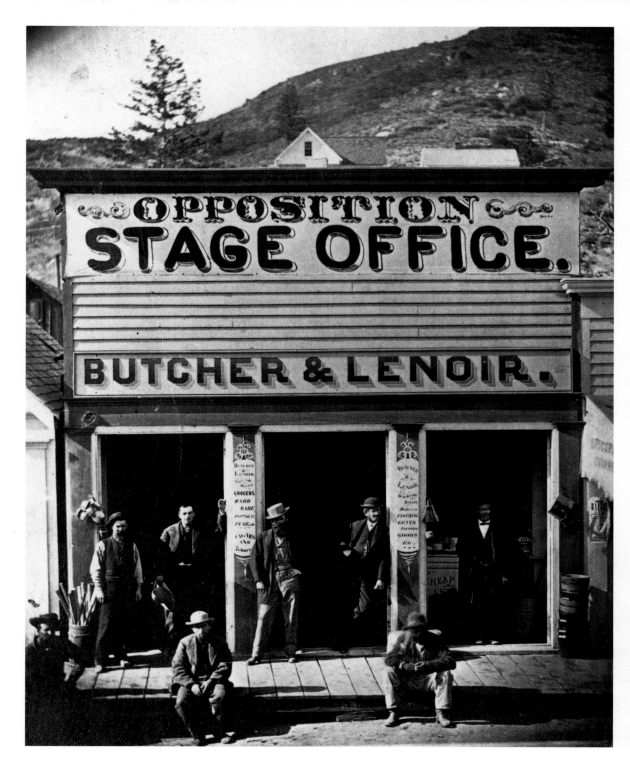

95 soldiers from Fort Boise to stop the fighting.

Along with other news of the day, the dramatic miners' disputes were reported in the *Owyhee Avalanche*, surely among the most colorful newspapers on the western frontier. One of its more memorable stories concerned Tom Cannivan, who was shot during a poker game. According to the *Avalanche* the miner's assailant, Daniel McIntosh, had been acquitted because of the poker hand Cannivan had been holding at the time of the ruckus. "Five queens are too many for one hand," the paper concluded. Even more memorable was the *Avalanche's* enumeration of the six basic types of drunks, providing a system of classification that was no doubt useful throughout the mining towns of the Wild West—and perhaps not completely irrelevant in more sophisticated social settings either:

"The first is ape-drunk. He leaps and sings and yells and dances, making all sorts of grimaces and cutting up all sorts of 'monkey-shines' to excite the laughter of his fellows. The second is tiger-drunk. He breaks the bottles, breaks the chairs, breaks the heads of fellow-carousers, and is full of blood and thunder. Of this sort are those who abuse their families. The third is hog-drunk. He rolls in the dirt on the floor, slobbers and grunts, and going into the streets makes his bed in the first ditch or filthy corner he may happen to fall into. He is heavy, lumpish and sleepy, and cries in a whining way for a little more drink. The fourth is puppy-drunk. He will weep for kindness, and whine his love and hug you in his arms, and kiss you with his slobbery lips, and proclaim how much he loves you. . . . The fifth is owl-drunk. He is wise in his own conceit. No man can differ with

him, for his word is law. . . . The sixth . . . is the fox-drunk man. He is crafty and ready to trade horses and cheat if he can. Keen to strike a bargain, leering round with low cunning, peeping through cracks, listening under the eaves, watching for some suspicious thing, sly as a fox, sneaking as the wolf. He is the meanest drunkard of them all."

Silver City prospered mightily for about a decade. Then came the Panic of 1873, and with it the collapse of the Bank of California, the financial institution that had helped fund the heavily

mechanized mining required by the diminishing lodes. Nevertheless, the richness of the ore kept the mines going, albeit at a reduced rate of profitability, until the end of World War II. Eighty-odd years is a long time for a mining town to exist, and Silver City's comet flew high and far. It is estimated that the mines in War Eagle Mountain produced some $40 million worth of ore during their eight decades of productivity.

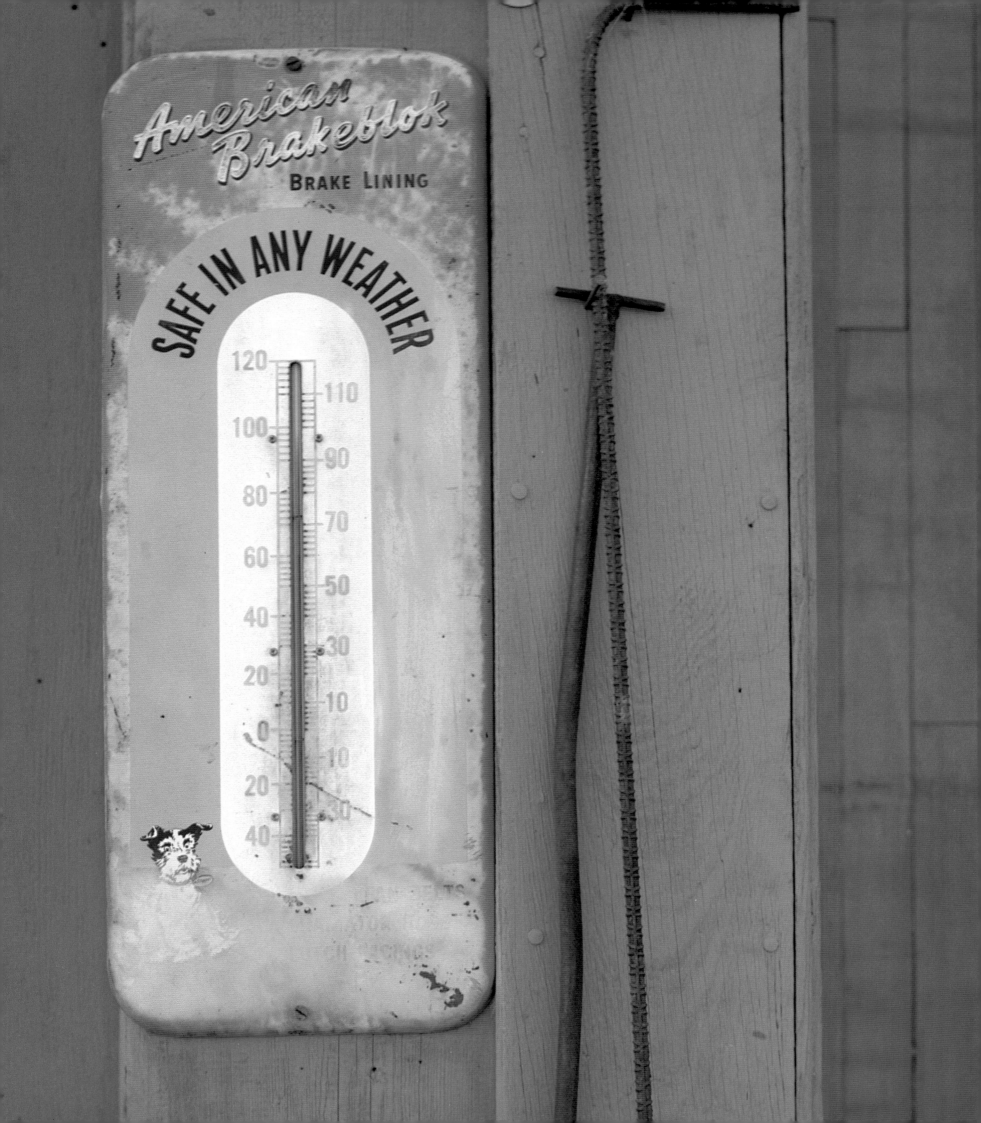

(Above) Molson, which began life as a mining town and then became a thriving farming community, is located on the rolling plains of northern Washington near the Canadian border.

(Opposite) Although the Molson schoolhouse serves as a formal museum, most of the town's buildings are open to visitors and many contain artifacts from the community's better days, such as this wall thermometer.

Molson, Washington, is a three-part town with a two-part history. Located in Okanagon County in the north central part of the state just a few miles south of the Canadian border, Molson first lived and died as a mining town. Then, responding to the promotional program of the Great Northern Railroad which sought to open up the agricultural potential of central Washington, it was reborn as a farming community. During its second incarnation, a feud over title to the land on which the town is located led to the establishment of no fewer than two rival Molsons.

Mining entrepreneur John W. Molson gave his money and his name to create the original town but never actually set foot in it. Its location and promotion was the responsibility of his partner, George B. Meacham, who went about his task with such a Barnum-like zest that he even produced a brochure showing settlers approaching the town via steamboats on Baker Creek, a tiny waterway that could barely support a canoe.

Meacham was not all talk. Armed with $75,000 of Molson's money, he located and laid out the town in 1900 to support the Poland China gold mine a few miles to the

This photo shows the remains of the commercial enterprises which fronted Main Street. Among them was the Sherling residence and law office building, seen in the foreground.

east. Within a year, he had erected a number of false-front wooden buildings and had a population of 300 living in them. Businesses included a general store and a drugstore, a post office was established, a dentist set up his practice, and of course the inevitable lawyer hung out his shingle. The pride of Molson, though, was the Tonasket Hotel, an impressive three-story structure with an outside balcony extending across the second facade and around one side.

Unfortunately, the Poland China mine soon gave out, and Molson the mining town passed into history.

The lifeblood of western railroads was western settlers, and much of the agricultural development of the American West during the late 19th century was undertaken in response to railroad promotion. At the very time Molson the mining town was being created, the Great Northern Railroad began a promotional campaign to lure settlers into central Washington. It was that campaign that gave Molson new life as a farming community.

Molson never entirely lost its residents, but during the brief hiatus between its life as a mining town and its life as a farming town, it did lose all of its commercial activity. Or at least that was the assertion of J. H. McDonald, who in 1905 filed a claim under the Homestead Act of 1862 for 160 acres, 40 of which included the former town of Molson. It turned out that all of the community's previous residents had neglected to seek legal title to the site and were simply squatters.

Led by Charles Blatt, the residents of the community contested the claim, pointing out that Molson, even in its moribund state, was a town, and a town was a commercial entity, which rendered it ineligible for homesteading. And besides that, they claimed, the area had never been surveyed, which was a necessary precondition for homesteading. Finally, out of desperation perhaps, Blatt filed a mining claim on the townsite, hoping somehow to conflict with McDonald's homestead bid.

The case wound its deliberate way through the court system until August 16, 1919, when a judge arrived at a creative decision worthy of King Solomon himself: he divided the claim, giving the citizens of Molson the 40 acres

(Below) It seems that the whole town of Molson turned out for the Fourth of July celebration in 1909. A highlight of the day was the bucking contest shown here.

(Bottom) The areas between buildings in Molson are scattered with old farm equipment and other historic relics.

upon which their town was located, and McDonald the outside 120 acres. Creative though the decision may have been, it failed to pacify some of the old-time Molsonites. W. W. Parry and Noah LaCass plotted a new townsite on LaCass' homestead north of town and moved into the "new" Molson.

The inevitable feud ensued. The population of the two communities could sustain only one school; which would get it? The same with the post office. And automobile dealerships and other businesses. A bank built in Old Molson was lifted onto skids and dragged over to New Molson, and for a time nobody knew for sure exactly where it would be open for business on any given day.

Another compromise was obviously necessary. It took the form of yet a third Molson, a "Central Molson" between the other two. The school was located there, and later the newspaper, the *Molson Leader*, edited and published by Howard and Georgia Mooney. The post office, the most hotly contested commodity between the two factions, followed shortly

(Top) Rapid communication—represented by this old telegraph office building—was particularly important in Molson during the years immediately following World War I when the community was one of the largest shippers of agricultural products in Washington State.

(Above) The interior of the Molson State Bank. During the feud between the competing communities, Old and New Molson, this building was placed on skids and dragged back and forth between the towns, leaving customers to hunt for it each day.

(Left) A homestead cabin built in 1908. It was J. H. McDonald's claim to the townsite under the Homestead Act of 1862 that led to Molson's division into three parts.

Construction materials which reflect various periods of Molson history range from old wood to brick—as in the Molson Mercantile Company building seen here—to recent wooden reconstructions.

thereafter, and as the heart of commercial and cultural activity began to rest upon Central Molson, peace at last arrived.

The story of the decline of Molson is the story of the decline of rural America. The town reached its peak shortly after World War I, when the Great Northern Railroad declared the country around the town to be the largest shipper of agricultural products in Washington north of Spokane. The agricultural depression of the 1920s hit the area hard, though, and Molson's fall was swift. By 1923 the Mooneys had moved their press to nearby Oroville, and in 1926 the Great Northern Railroad discontinued service to the area. Farm families moved away, and cattle ranchers purchased their land for grazing.

Molson today is in the midst of livestock, not farming, country, as far-ranging cattle grazing on native grasses have replaced the overly optimistic dreams of agricultural empire. Of the three Molsons, many of the old buildings remain to tell the town's two-part history, while an outdoor museum of mule-powered farm machinery reminds space-age visitors of another time's failed dreams.

The Southwest

(Above) The ruins of a mine structure and assorted buildings at Golden, in the hill country of northern New Mexico.

(Opposite) This close-up shows the type of rough-hewn log construction that was common in mining town buildings during the 1880s.

(Previous pages) A lone rider and his dog survey the remains of Cabezon, New Mexico.

The riches of Golden, New Mexico, passed through the hands of two gold-hungry nations—Spain and Mexico—before the Americans finally discovered its elusive hiding place. Like much of the Southwest, its history is the story of two worlds—the Hispanic and the Anglo-American.

Gold was the great lure that brought the Spanish conquistadors into the often inhospitable regions of the American Southwest. After they had captured the immense wealth of Peru's Incas and Mexico's Aztecs, they had pressed northward in search of the precious metal, a quest that brought them as far as present-day Arizona, New Mexico, and Utah. The gold of what became the southwestern United States remained elusive, however, until the area's settlements joined with their southern sisters in a Mexico that was independent of Spain. Even then, the Mexicans eked out little return for their prospecting efforts, and it fell to the Americans, after the Mexican War of 1846–1848, to mine the great bounties of southwestern gold.

The first significant strikes were made by a Spanish herder in the Ortiz Mountains northeast of Albuquerque about 1828. This area, known as the Old Placers, produced

well enough for over a decade, but it was quickly abandoned about 1840 when a nearby district, which became known as the New Placers, began yielding even greater riches from ore dross. Accordingly, burros were used to bring ore from the mountains to the valley where it was washed in a small stream. *Bateas*, or crude wooden vessels functioning as gold pans, were the only newcomers decided to change the name of the community to Golden.

The 1880s gold boom that resulted from the importation of better machinery and refining techniques lasted only

Within the image: 23. GOLD MINING WITH DRY-WASHER, GOLDEN, N.M.

(Above) This intrepid miner is working his claim in Golden using a dry washer. By 1895, when this photo was taken, such primitive means had largely given way to more sophisticated technology and lone prospectors had been replaced by large mining companies.

(Opposite) The Franciscan mission church is a reconstructed adobe structure that was originally built in the early 19th century.

Stories that the San Pedro Mountains contained $800 million in gold attracted large numbers of miners, but investors remained wary. The owners of the Canyon del Agua & San Pedro eventually decided, as many businesses since then have done, that an endorsement from a well-known public figure would probably loosen investors' purse strings. Accordingly, they made the Civil War hero and ex-president Ulysses S. Grant the president of their company and brought him out to Santa Fe to inspect some of the ore. Although Grant's knowledge of mining was virtually nil, he encouraged investors to buy stock in the company. What Grant didn't know about mining, he compensated for with a painful knowledge of inflated stock values acquired during the corrupt years of his presidential administration. When equities in the Canyon del Agua & San Pedro skyrocketed immediately after his endorsement, he quickly resigned before lawyers and investors could take a closer look at the company's assets.

At its peak in the early 1880s, Golden was an incongruous combination of sleepy Spanish mission and western boomtown. With a population of perhaps 400, the community had its own newspaper, a stage station, a blacksmith, a shoemaker, a lawyer, and the two-story Palace Hotel. Overlooking this urban bustle was the old church of San Francisco, a crude adobe structure that seemed the very embodiment of the austerity and penitential demeanor of the Franciscan order, surrounded by the bleached headstones of its *camposanto*, or graveyard.

By modern standards 400 people is not much of a town, but Golden took itself seriously as a community. Col. R. K. Webb, who operated Golden's newspaper, *The Retort,* was a fearless journalistic crusader who would have been at home in cities many times the size of Golden. Webb spoke out dramatically against the corrupt, Gilded-Age corporate practices of the Canyon del Agua & San Pedro, which had cavalierly crowded out smaller competitors to monopolize the mines. Webb's editorials may have had an effect on public opinion, for in May 1883 a group of citizens took over the company's mine and refused to allow operations to continue until harassment against its smaller competitors ceased.

After 1884, Golden's prosperity declined as the ore bodies tapered off, and by 1900 its population had almost disappeared. The Palace Hotel burned in 1890, and by then there were so few transients that it was never restored. The church of San Francisco, though, was more fortunate. In 1910, Fray Angelico Chavez, who was assigned to the mission district south of Santa Fe, largely rebuilt the ancient church. Although the foundation is about the only part of the original structure that he was able to retain, the restoration is faithful to the original style of the building and may be considered an authentic Spanish mission. Today, as one looks over the ruins of the dozen or so structures from the town's mining period, history seems to have come full circle. For, thanks to the restoration of the neat little church, El Real de San Francisco has returned to its original purpose.

91

The Franciscan mission church, which can
be seen in the distance in this photo, occupies
a commanding position overlooking the ruins
of Golden, New Mexico.

(*Below*) Fray Angelico Chavez was the principal force behind the re-creation of Golden's ancient church of San Francisco, which can be seen on page 90 and in the distance of the photo at left.

(*Right*) structure in this photo suggests, from the nearby hills provided a viable supplement to the area's principal building materials—adobe and logs.

(Above) Originally called La Posta, Cabezon was a small mining town. It also served as a relay station for the stagecoach line that carried passengers from Santa Fe to Fort Wingate.

(Opposite) Cabezon today is one of the Southwest's finest ghost towns. Its "eerie silence of total desolation," as one book puts it, makes a visit here truly memorable.

The culture of the American Southwest is a creative mixture of Indian, Hispanic, and Anglo-American elements. Cabezon, New Mexico, located northwest of Albuquerque, is an almost classic example of the intertwining of those cultures.

The number four has sacred significance in the Navajo religion, and the Indians define the boundaries of their homeland by four sacred mountains and four sacred rivers. One of the latter is the Rio Puerco, a western tributary of the Rio Grande. When, in the early 1870s, Hispanic settlers created a small community called La Posta on its bank, they were aware that the site had both geographic and religious significance for the Navajos.

La Posta was located in the shadow of Cabezon Peak, which the Navajo call the "Giant's Head." According to tribal legend, the Twin War Brothers, heroic figures in Navajo mythology, killed a giant at nearby Mt. Taylor. The dried blood of the giant gave rise to the lava beds at Grants, New Mexico, and the place where the massive severed head came to rest—40 miles east of the battle site—became Cabezon Peak, *cabezón* being Spanish for "big head."

Although they acknowledged Navajo tradition, the Hispanic intruders were not welcomed by the Indians. In the decades prior to the establishment of La Posta, the Navajo repeatedly chased them back across the river. It was not until 1864 that the celebrated mountain man and scout Kit Carson and the U.S. army defeated the Navajo and opened the area for settlement.

La Posta, the first permanent community beneath Cabezon Peak, was a small mining town that also served as a stop for fresh horses along the stage route from Santa Fe to Fort Wingate. The main economic base of the community, though, was farming; livestock

had ample room to graze on the vast plain watered by the Rio Puerco. In 1891, the town was awarded a post office and the name was changed to Cabezon.

Two Anglos, John Pflueger and Richard F. Heller, were attracted by the economic potential of Cabezon. Not only was it strategically located along a major transportation route, but its countryside offered lucrative agricultural possibilities. Consequently, in 1888, Pflueger and Heller opened a general store and were soon accepted by their Navajo and Hispanic neighbors. Pfleuger eventually sold his interests to Heller and moved away, but Heller stayed for the rest of his long life. The growth and prosperity of Cabezon were both largely a result of

This old residence later became a dance hall. By 1915 the population of Cabezon had grown to about 375, and the town boasted four stores, several saloons, a post office, a church, and a school.

his business acumen and his promotional abilities.

Heller became the biggest livestock man in the area. His holdings, at their height, included some 2,000 cattle and 10,000 sheep. So vast in fact was his empire that it took as many as 40 wagons to transport his annual wool production to market. Heller employed a number of Navajo teamsters and herdsmen, and tribal members were cus-

The small cemetery beside La Iglesia de San José holds some two dozen graves, dating from the latter portion of the 19th century to the current era. Several of them are marked with architecturally distinctive head-stones, such as the one in the foreground of this photo.

(Top) Although Hispanics attempted to colonize the area that would eventually give rise to Cabezon, New Mexico, it was not until 1864 that celebrated mountain man and scout Kit Carson, pictured here, and the U.S. army defeated the Navajo and opened the area for settlement.

(Above) The town's leading citizen, Richard Heller (right), posed for this photograph, circa 1890–1909, with his wife, dog, and assistant. After Heller died in 1947, Mrs. Heller continued to run the town's post office for a time and then moved to Albuquerque.

tomers as well. Because the Indians mistrusted paper money, most of his business transactions were made in hard currency. Of the 40 wagons that went to market, one would return heavily laden with coins of gold and silver. Perhaps because of the large numbers of Navajo who guarded those returns, there is no record of bandits ever having waylaid the money wagon.

Heller's role as a positive force in the community can hardly be overestimated, for it went far beyond his economic contribution. For one thing, the town lacked a hotel, so Heller and his wife often opened their 11-room home to stranded wayfarers. Also, in an attempt to attract settlers and to enhance the stability of the community, Heller built a large church, La Iglesia de San José, for the Roman Catholic diocese.

In spite of Heller's best efforts, though, Cabezon never achieved great prosperity or urban importance. In 1897 the town had a population of about 100, but the school only functioned three months out of the year, and Mass was said in the church only once a year. By 1915 the population had grown to about 375, and the town had, in addition to the church and school, four stores, some saloons and dance halls, and the post office. But shortly thereafter the town collapsed.

Transportation, livestock, and agriculture would seem to have offered a more permanent economic base than an extractive industry like mining, and in fact Cabezon proved unable to hang onto that base and faded away completely as a mining town. But its role as a transportation hub was damaged, first, when a 1920s branch line of the Santa Fe Railroad bypassed the town and, later, when modern highways chose more direct routes across New

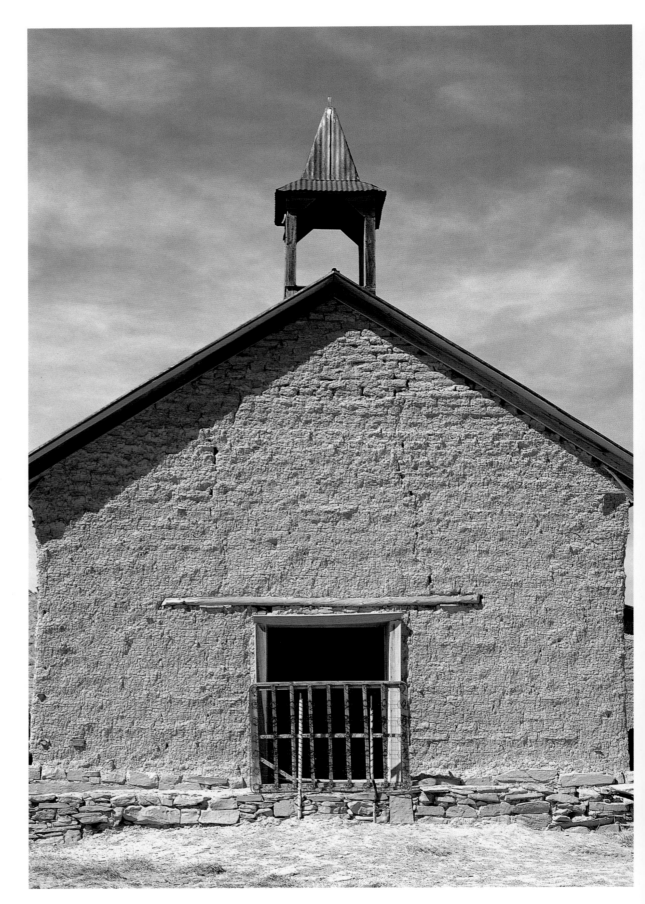

In an effort to attract settlers to the Cabezon area and to enhance the stability of the community, Richard F. Heller built a large church, La Iglesia de San José, for the Roman Catholic diocese.

(**Previous pages**) Cabezon, New Mexico, is located near Cabezon Peak, called the "Giant's Head" by the Navajo. Tribal legend holds that the mountain was formed from the severed head of a huge mythical being.

100

(Above) This store marked the start of Richard Heller's empire, which eventually included some 2,000 cattle and 10,000 sheep. So vast were his holdings that it took as many as 40 wagons to transport his annual wool production to market.

(Right) Sheep graze in the shadow of Cabezon Peak in a photo taken some time between 1890 and 1924. The timelessness of the area is suggested by the 34-year span attributed to this image.

Mexico than had the old stage line that gave Cabezon its life.

Another knockout blow was administered by the U.S. government, which decided in 1934 that livestock grazing had destroyed the Rio Puerco bottomlands. The Taylor Grazing Act of that year brought the whole area of the old Spanish Ojo del Espíritu Santo land grant, which encompassed the Rio Puerco drainage, under control of the newly created Bureau of Land Management. The BLM observed that overgrazing had caused erosion and a deepening of the channel of the Rio Puerco to a point where getting its water up to the farmlands was becoming difficult. It believed that the continuing existence of agriculture in the area was in danger unless grazing was immediately and severely restricted. As if to confirm the BLM's assessment, the Rio Puerco, swollen by spring rainwater unrestrained by vegetation on the overgrazed terrain, wiped out several dams designed to divert water for irrigation. Thus, agriculture and grazing

came to an end in Cabezon almost simultaneously.

Then, in 1947, Richard Heller, who had carried the community on his shoulders for almost 60 years, died. His widow continued to run the post office for a year, but then she gave up and moved to Albuquerque. With her departure, the post office closed and the town gradually became deserted. Cabezon today is one of the Southwest's finest ghost towns. Its "eerie silence of total desolation," as one book puts it, makes a visit a truly memorable experience. The church and its graveyard, the dusty streets, the dozen or so ruined buildings, and Cabezon Peak looming in the background give the place a unique, ghostly atmosphere. Readers are cautioned, though, that Cabezon is on private property and permission to enter it may well be difficult to obtain. Vandalism has caused considerable damage to some of the structures, and the current owners, deeply concerned about the town's future, do not encourage tourist stopovers.

The interior of La Iglesia de San José. By 1897, the town's population was approaching 100, but school was in session only three months out of the year and Mass was said in the church only once annually.

Although Cabezon was something of a transportation hub, the community's main economic base came from farming; livestock had ample room to graze in the vast plain watered by the Rio Puerco.

(*Above*) Today fewer than a dozen buildings remain on Avon Avenue, the main street of Shakespeare, New Mexico, but in the 1880s this was a bustling—if somewhat dangerous—thoroughfare.

(*Opposite*) The crumbling remains of this saloon almost lead one to expect that at any moment a cowpoke is going to pull up a chair, take a swig from the bottle, and start to deal the cards.

The history of Shakespeare, New Mexico, offers ample evidence of the wilder aspects of the Wild West. With a famous stagecoach line, fierce Apache Indians, a rich silver mine, a diamond hoax, a suicide, hangings, desperadoes, and a red-light district, Shakespeare is a ghost-town aficionado's paradise.

Although the town's economic base during its heyday came from the rich silver ore in the nearby Pyramid Mountains, the area's first settlers were attracted to the region by a much more fundamental commodity, one particularly rare in extreme southwestern New Mexico: water.

Originally known as Mexican Springs, the site was first used as an alternate station for the Butterfield Overland Mail in the 1850s. Stage service ceased during the Civil War, but John Evenson and Jack Frost, two scouts for the National Mail and Transportation Company, reestablished a stage station at the site after the war, naming it Grant after the victorious Union general. For a while it seemed that Grant would become part of the route for the transcontinental railroad when those conducting the Pacific Railroad Survey of 1853 along the 32nd parallel passed close to the site. That route was not chosen, how-

ever. Nor for that matter were any of the others surveyed by the federal government. But W. D. Brown, a surveyor working on the team that visited Mexican Springs, discovered something in the area of considerably greater value than a location for a railroad depot. Poking around in the Pyramid Mountains, he pocketed several samples of high-grade ore that assayed in San Francisco at 12,000 ounces of silver per ton.

Brown sought out William C. Ralston, founder of the Bank of California, and in 1870, Harpending and Company, the venture that they formed, showed up at Grant, New Mexico, with plans to make its fortune in the Pyramid Mountains. Soon an impressive

tent city with six streets grew up around the depot. The new town, the new economic base, and the new financial benefactor seemed to dictate a new name as well, and Grant became Ralston, New Mexico.

Its namesake, William Ralston, had plenty of money—or at least knew how to raise it—but his attention to detail seems to have been lacking. After laying a general claim to the mining district around his new town, he ran off to England to raise additional funds among potential investors there. Unfortunately, his claims had not been properly staked and, while he was away, newcomers to Ralston were able to jump many of them. Worse, some of the claims on which he had placed his highest hopes proved to be only isolated ore pockets, not the rich veins he had expected.

Ralston's investments were in serious jeopardy, and his fear of losing everything seems to have rendered him vulnerable to an even shakier scheme than the silver mine. Philip Arnold and John Slack, two prospectors, salted an area near Ralston with diamonds and got a respected mining engineer, Henry Janin, to verify what appeared to be a bona fide diamond mine. Hoping to recoup his silver losses, Ralston bought into the diamond scheme and took additional investors with him. The diamond mine was revealed as a hoax in 1872, when geologist Clarence King—investigating another Janin report of a diamond mine, this time in

(Right) Although this photo looks like it was taken in the 1890s, it in fact comes from about 1960. The Stratford Hotel, which can be seen at right, is believed to have been an early employer of a dishwasher known as Billy Antrim. He later became known as William Bonney, alias Billy the Kid.

(Below) The interior of the old mail station. Shakespeare was a stopping point for the Butterfield Overland Mail, which carried letters, packages, and passengers across the West during the 1850s.

the Uinta Mountains of northern Utah—proved the Ralston site had been salted.

Ralston was at least an honest—if not a wise—businessman, and he paid back all investment losses from his mining ventures out of his own pocket. Unfortunately, he had just completed these refunds when the Panic of 1873 struck and wiped out even his Bank of California. Perhaps it was Ralston's suicidal despondency over his financial losses that led to his drowning in San Francisco Bay in 1875.

Meanwhile, back in New Mexico, there were others who continued to pursue the rich silver veins that had eluded Ralston. Col. John Boyle from St. Louis staked some new claims in the late 1870s for the Shakespeare Mining Company and made them pay

better than any of those worked by Ralston's firm. In order to avoid gloomy associations with William Ralston in the minds of potential investors, Boyle thought it wise to change the town's name yet again. Accordingly, in 1879, Ralston became Shakespeare, New Mexico, after the company that was leading its resurrection.

The population of Shakespeare was smaller than that of Ralston, and thus a simpler town layout seemed appropriate. Instead of the three main streets and three cross streets that the earlier town had featured, Shakespeare was laid out along one main thoroughfare, Avon Avenue. There were about 200 Shakespeareans in 1884, and the adobe buildings of the town housed three saloons, a couple of hotels, and a smattering of other businesses. There was

also a "suburban" area in the northwest called Poverty Flat. It was the red-light district.

The 1880s were the most colorful period of Shakespeare's history. Apache marauders became such a threat that the town formed its own militia of 70 men, known as the Shakespeare Guard. Vigilant though it was, the Guard was unable to prevent the occasional Indian attack. During one such raid, a band of Apache killed a judge named

(Opposite) **There were two hotels in Shakespeare during the 1880s, one of which, the Stratford, is seen here. These hostelries were badly needed because the town served as a way station for the Overland Stage line and a terminus for a spur of the Southern Pacific Railroad.**

(Below) **Originally called Mexican Springs, Shakespeare's role as a transportation hub derived from its abundance of water.**

(Above) The porch of the general store. Many of the buildings in Shakespeare are furnished with artifacts from the town's boom days.

(Right) Most of the buildings in Shakespeare are constructed of adobe bricks, which give the town an authentic southwestern atmosphere.

The noose hanging from the ceiling in the Grant House hotel is a macabre reminder of a double lynching that took place here during the town's heyday. One morning, stage passengers discovered the bodies of the dead men when they arrived at the hotel for breakfast.

McComas and his wife and kidnapped their son Charles. In spite of pursuit by the Shakespeare Guard and a proffered reward for return of the boy, he was never seen again.

On occasion Shakespeare was also visited by desperadoes of the type featured in lurid western novels and films. Once an outlaw named Sandy King shot off the index finger of a Shakespeare clerk at Smyth's Mercantile Store while his partner, Russian Bill, stole a horse and headed east toward Deming. Later a posse of two found Bill in an empty boxcar and brought him back to Shakespeare for punishment. He never made it to trial, however. A lynch mob hanged him and his partner from the ceiling beams of the large Grant House Hotel, perhaps for lack of nearby trees of suitable size, or perhaps to make conspicuous examples of the outlaws. Their bodies continued to dangle from the hotel rafters the following day, where they were discovered by hungry stagecoach passengers as they rushed into the Grant House for breakfast.

Mining in Shakespeare continued to be an off-and-on affair, with the town's prosperity fluctuating accordingly. During the 1890s most of the mines closed, but some opened again in 1907 and the town struggled to find new life. Even after mining ceased entirely, the town enjoyed a brief period of prosperity as a whistle stop for the Southern Pacific Railroad. One of its spur lines ran right down Avon Avenue to connect with the mines at Valedon to the south. The Great Depression of the 1930s finally brought an end to the industries that had been at the root of Shakespeare's economy throughout its many incarnations—mining and transport—and the town's only income today comes from its lure as a tourist attraction.

(Above) Jerome, Arizona, is situated on the steep hillside of Mingus Mountain. At its peak in 1925, it had a population of 15,000, making it the fourth largest city in Arizona at the time.

(Opposite) Numerous pieces of mining equipment are on display at Jerome. This stamp mill, for example, was used to crush ore in order to separate copper compounds from the surrounding rock.

In its heyday, the copper mining community of Jerome, Arizona, seemed to grow by inverse direction: as its economic fortunes soared skyward, the town itself began slipping down the steep hillside on which it was built. Unfortunately the economy eventually went into decline as well, but while the town's fortunes leveled off, the town itself continued to go downhill—literally—into the 1940s.

What gave rise to the town and its initial good fortune were the rich copper deposits in Mingus Mountain, the central Arizona peak on which Jerome is situated. Ancient ruins in the area datable to 935 A.D. indicate that the Tuzigoot Indians had utilized the brilliant blue azurite for body paint and pottery decoration long before the advent of European explorers. During the 16th century, two Spanish parties visited the Tuzigoot mine shaft—one led by Antonio de Espejo in 1583, and the other under Marcos Farfan de los Godos in 1598. But they scorned the copper deposits and continued their search for gold.

It was Al Sieber, a scout for the famous Apache fighter Gen. George Crook, who first realized the value of the copper. Unfortunately he lacked the capital necessary to do

113

anything about it, and so did M. A. Ruffner and Angus McKinnon, who filed a claim in the area the same year. The mining boom began when Ruffner and McKinnon convinced the Arizona governor, Frederick E. Tritle, of the value of the site and sold their claim to him for $15,000. Tritle secured financial backing from New York capitalists James A. MacDonald and Eugene Jerome and began working the claim as the United Verde Copper Company. Jerome, incidentally, may have been less interested in mining than in having a town named for him, for that was a precondition of his investment.

In the light of its eventual wealth, the United Verde Copper Company had a curiously rocky beginning. Formed in 1882, it had barely commenced operations when the copper market went into a slump and the mine shut down. Fortunately, Sen. William A. Clark of Montana became attracted to the United Verde, bought it out, and reopened the mine on an expanded scale. Major fires in three successive years—1897, 1898, and 1899—created temporary setbacks, but the mines were paying well by that time and the city of Jerome was incorporated in 1899.

The term "city" is appropriate, for during the early 20th century Jerome was the fourth largest town in Arizona. Its commercial, professional, and cultural life ran the entire gamut, from grocery and hardware stores to saloons and restaurants, with doctors, lawyers, dentists, and even photographers plying their professions in the community. There was a massive school with a colonnaded facade that looked as though it had been built to last forever, and the large stone Montana Hotel boasted lodgings for 1,000 single men in what was perhaps the largest building in Arizona.

Like many western mining towns that grew up during the great immigration boom of the late 19th and early 20th centuries, Jerome boasted a population with a variety of ethnic and national backgrounds, each having its own residential district. In addition to

Jerome had a genuine urban splendor uncharacteristic of mining towns. A hotel like the one pictured here could lodge up to 1,000 single men.

(Opposite) The ruins of a bank. Although Jerome has a substantial population today and many of its buildings have been restored, some structures have unstable foundations and may be entered only with special permission.

114

the Hispanic and Anglo miners that one would expect to find in Arizona, there were miners from Wales and Sweden and surprisingly large numbers of immigrants from eastern and southern Europe—Slavs and Italians.

While the niceties of modern urban planning had little, if any, effect upon Jerome's development, the city's high vantage point offered a striking view of Verde Valley with Oak Creek Canyon in the distance. Moreover, the steepness of the hillside meant that one's view was usually unobstructed by a neighbor's roof. But the hill's incline also made the town rather difficult to traverse. With only one main street winding around the gradation, much of the crosstown traffic proceeded by means of steep wooden stairways.

Jerome's geography became even more complicated during the 1920s,

when the whole community began to slip downward. The shift resulted from several causes, including the inherent instability of the town's montainous locale, whose surface of loose rock and soil covered a foundation of solid rock. In addition the large Verde Fault ran through Mingus Mountain and beneath the town. Added to these geological factors were some 88 miles of tunnels under the town and the regular use of dynamite to expose new ore deposits. Given these conditions, it is little wonder, as one historian has put it, that "Jerome progressed downward as well as ahead." During one famous episode, spectators in a movie theater chose to ignore the tremors they experienced—as all residents of Jerome had learned to do—and continued to watch the film. But when they tried to leave the building to go home, they found the sidewalk—which had been only a

few inches above the threshold when they had entered the theater—some 2 feet above ground. The building had virtually sunk into the earth in a few minutes.

The economy of Jerome eventually slipped just as the town did. Labor conflicts arose shortly after the turn of the century, calling attention to the exploitative policies of the United Verde management. The first strike, in 1907, did gain a raise for the miners—to $2.75 per day—and the reduction of the work day from 10 to 8 hours. Another strike was attempted in 1917, but it failed to generate widespread support among the miners. In the aftermath, 67 militant labor activists and organizers were forcibly deported from the town's environs.

The Great Depression was no kinder

to Jerome than it was to most other American communities. Copper prices dropped drastically, and in 1932 the United Verde mines ceased operations. Jerome gained a temporary respite in 1935 when the large Phelps-Dodge Corporation bought out United Verde and resumed production, but it too ceased operations in 1950 and many workers left to seek new opportunities elsewhere. Soon, of the 15,000 inhabitants who had lived in the community at the peak of its prosperity in 1925, only about 100 remained.

Whatever economic vitality Jerome has today comes from its appeal to tourists, for it is Arizona's largest "historic community under restoration," as the locals prefer to call it, and it boasts a fine museum of mining equipment. Many visitors come, too, to measure visually the physical descent of the town down Mingus Mountain and perhaps to philosophize about the parallel with its economic misfortunes.

New York capitalist Eugene M. Jerome was one of the principals in the United Verde Copper Company, which was formed to exploit the rich copper deposits in the mountains of central Arizona. Jerome insisted that the town to which their mine operations gave rise be named for him.

(Above) Smelter workers for the United Verde mine posed for this photograph around the turn of the century. Within a few years, labor disputes between the miners and the United Verde operators would dramatically change this tranquil scene.

(Left) Beyond the old school in the foreground of this photo, one can get a glimpse of Verde Valley. The steepness of the mountain on which Jerome sits makes a spectacular view possible from almost any point in town.

Mining at Jerome began in ancient times and lasted well into the age of mechanized technology.

(Below) Even some of Jerome's unrestored structures, like the Little Daisy Hotel seen here in close-up, bear evidence of their past elegance.

The Far West

(Above) The giant Joshua tree in front of the post office in Gold Point provided a welcome respite from the heat (Death Valley is only a few miles away) and enhanced the post office's value as a social center.

(Opposite) An old chair outside the Gold Point post office. The post office in any small town is a natural gathering place, and one can imagine Gold Point miners seated in chairs like this one discussing the events of the day.

(Previous pages) An ore cart at the Berlin Mill in Berlin, Nevada.

It was not uncommon for a western town to be reborn in another guise, often with another name, after an exhausted economic base was replaced by a productive one. Perhaps the most telling example of this phenomenon was Gold Point, Nevada. It has had so many resurrections under so many names that it reminds one of the proverbial cat with nine lives.

Its first incarnation, which was not very impressive either in income or urban dimensions, came in 1868, when lime deposits were discovered in Slate Ridge, not far over the Nevada border from Death Valley, California. Lime is an important product, but not one to compete in profitability with serious concentrations of precious metals. Nevertheless, the find was lucrative enough to give rise to a small town called Lime Point, which was founded at the northern base of the ridge.

Things changed dramatically for Lime Point in 1880 when large deposits of hornsilver were discovered near the lime quarries. Hornsilver, or cerargyrite, is a chloride compound containing 75 percent silver, obviously a very high concentration. A brief mining boom followed this discovery, and the town gained its first significant population. It

also gained the second of its names—Hornsilver.

The boom was brief because the difficulty and expense of milling the ore, high though it was in silver content, precluded extended activity. The nearest mill to the town was in Lida, roughly 20 miles to the northwest and reachable only by means of a sandy desert road that was nearly impossible to traverse. Besides its inaccessibility, the mill was very inefficient, so the effort to haul ore to it was hardly worthwhile. By 1882, problems with the mill had reached the point where the mines at Hornsilver were virtually abandoned pending development of a better, closer facility or improved transportation to more remote ones.

The development of the town of Tonopah by the end of the century led to a brief revival of the Hornsilver mines, for ore could be shipped from there on the railroad. But Tonopah was even further than Lida, and much of the miners' profits were ground into those sandy roads. When the big gold strikes occurred in Goldfield, Nevada, in 1903/04, Hornsilver miners generally gave up their Slate Ridge claims and moved north to the bigger digs.

A few stubborn souls stayed, however, and they later reaped their reward. In 1905, the Great Western mine commenced operations in Hornsilver, and in 1908 its miners discovered even greater concentrations of hornsilver than those they had been working. Many of the Goldfield deserters began to return and found themselves joined by hundreds of newcomers.

This boom put Hornsilver on the map as never before. Its history during this period is particularly well-documented, because its newspaper, the *Hornsilver Herald*, began publication

In 1908, during the hornsilver boom, two 4-horse teams and one 16-mule team were kept busy hauling lumber over immense distances so that houses like the one shown here could be built.

only two weeks after the boom began. Like most boomtown newspapers, the *Herald* was not backward in trumpeting the town's lucrative prospects. In the very first issue, the editor predicted Hornsilver's impending preeminence among Nevada mining communities—truly an ambitious forecast in a state that had produced the Comstock Lode!

He was right, though, in predicting that Hornsilver's best years lay in the future. Already, in 1908, he could point to 220 houses and an estimated population of 700. The M. A. Maher Company was running two 4-horse teams and one 16-mule team constantly to haul lumber for new buildings. No fewer than eight boarding

During its heyday, Gold Point had a population of several hundred people. A few residents remain, still working mines in the nearby hills, but most of the old houses are empty of both people and furniture.

houses and restaurants existed along with several stores. Plans were under way to pipe water in from Lida. The town even had an entertainment committee, and it had just staged a "Grand Ball" at the Lime Point Restaurant.

Not all of Hornsilver's growing pains were happy, however. The combination of exuberant miners and the ready availability of alcohol soon created the need for a jail, or at least a drunk tank. But the town didn't have one. Accordingly, when one reveler overindulged, the deputy sheriff, M. J. Spaulding, had to improvise. "In the absence of a jail," said the *Herald*, "Mr. Spaulding handcuffed said citizen to the rear wheel of a huge freight wagon, where the party remained until he was able to more fully understand himself."

Despite its boisterous denizens, Hornsilver continued to grow. Soon the *Herald* was boasting of the construction of a new hotel. Two stories in height with 10,000 square feet, the building had 33 rooms, an office, a bar, and a dining room that measured an impressive 20 feet by 30 feet. This "superior class" structure was a model of the latest construction techniques, including double walls insulated with building paper "insuring warmth and being dust proof," the *Herald* proudly reported. Anyone who has lived in the Nevada desert might dispute the ability of any material to keep out the dust, but one can still be impressed by Hornsilver's developing urban sophistication.

In 1908, when this photo was taken, Hornsilver (as the town was then called) was in the midst of a great boom. The rise in the community's fortunes came with the discovery of significant concentrations of hornsilver, a chloride compound containing 75 percent silver.

The editor of the *Herald* was understandably optimistic about the future of his community, and his enthusiasm didn't seem without foundation. Corroborative evidence regarding Hornsilver's progress could be found in the Goldfield newspapers as well. "The town is growing faster than any new camp that has been discovered in this section," one paper reported, "and additions to the original townsite are being laid off in all directions." "Hornsilver is the latest wonder in Nevada mining districts!" another exulted, nearly exceeding even the *Herald's* enthusiasm. "Hornsilver is a comer! . . . New mercantile concerns are coming in every week . . . and Main Street is extending in length almost as you watch it."

But Hornsilver's Main Street, as well as its mines, reached a zenith in 1909, and then once again the town fell into decline as the pockets of ore began to diminish and the dwindling profits from those that continued to produce were eaten up by legal fees resulting from conflicting mining claims. Although some deposits remained, the mills that had refined the richer ore simply couldn't make the poorer ores pay. In 1915, even the Great Western mine, Hornsilver's most profitable operation, which had produced a reported half-million dollars during the preceding decade, went into a receivership headed by Charles Stoneham, owner of the New York Giants baseball team.

But Hornsilver was not yet dead. By 1930, the silver mines were producing gold! The town's fortunes seemed to warrant yet a third name change, and thus Hornsilver became Gold Point. The new town enjoyed substantial prosperity until the beginning of World War II. But, in October 1942, as workers left the area to labor in the more important and lucrative war industries located elsewhere, the Gold Point mines ceased operation.

And still the town refused to die. During the late 1980s, local residents and some enterprising outsiders decided that Gold Point's real gold was not in the ground; it was in tourists' credit cards. The result was a significant construction boom designed to introduce modern amenities into the town's old buildings and to make a visit to Gold Point both entertaining and comfortable. From lime to silver to gold to tourism is not quite nine lives, but Gold Point is not finished yet.

Gold Point's Main Street features some of the sandy, desolate terrain that made transportation in and out of the community difficult and long retarded the town's development.

(Above) Gold Point boasted significant urban luxuries despite its remote location. No doubt many a surprised traveler spent an unexpectedly good night here in a bed with a brass headstand like the one in this photo.

(Left) The domestic utensils and bottles in the general store add up to an impressive collection. Although most buildings in Gold Point are vacant, some feature displays of artifacts like the one pictured here.

(Above) Located off of Route 82 in Nye County, Nevada, Belmont contains the remains of what was once a thriving mining town.

(Opposite) As the sheriff's office in the courthouse attests, vandalism has been a major problem in Belmont. Several exceptional buildings have even been torn down by destructive visitors.

Nevada Highway 8A stretches a long 150 miles from Tonopah to Austin, and travelers who do not turn aside on Highway 82 to visit the ruins of Belmont will have little on the journey to break the monotony of a trek through rather barren, undistinguished country. Those who do will find the well-preserved remains of a city of 2,000 that at one time was the seat of Nye County, Nevada.

Like many mining towns, Belmont sprang up suddenly. A nameless Indian first reported silver ore in the Toquima Range in October 1865. Miners from nearby Ione confirmed the wealth of the strike, and the following year a rush to the area from other mining camps began. It was about as close to the discovery of a new Comstock Lode as Nevada was ever to see: surface ores assayed at between $200 and $3,000 worth of silver per ton, and during its 20-year heyday, the mines in the new Silver Bend District produced some $15 million.

Wealth like that could support the construction of a pretty impressive city, especially when building materials were inexpensively available close by. In Belmont's first two years, no fewer than five sawmills were erected in the Toquimas to provide lumber for the booming community. A high grade of clay was discovered a few miles from town, and bricks manufactured in three kilns were used for the construction of some of the town's most impressive buildings. Stone, too, was used. It was plentifully available in the nearby mountains. The result was a substantially built community that almost from the beginning gave an impression of prosperity and permanence.

Nye County had been created in 1864, more as a definable geographic expanse than a population center, for the small mining community of Ione was its only town. Ione naturally became the first county seat, but it was also natural that once Belmont was established the new boomtown would challenge its neighbor for that honor. That challenge came in 1867, and the state legislature awarded the prize to Belmont. However, the taxpayers of Nye County, who had just paid for a courthouse at Ione, made Belmont the new county seat seven years before they agreed to finance another one there.

In the meantime, Belmont quickly developed into a diverse and urbane community. No fewer than three newspapers, the *Belmont Courier*, the *Silver Bend Reporter*, and the *Mountain Champion*, competed for Belmont readers. Those with more cosmopolitan tastes had only to visit H. P. Stimler's Belmont News Depot, where other Nevada and California papers were available. Like many other frontier journalists, Belmont editors were both witty and straightforward in their opinions. "Here's to our governor," the *Reporter* once cheered. "He came in with very little opposition; he goes out with none at all."

Immigrant labor brought ethnic diversity to Belmont as it did to other mining towns. After completion of the

At Belmont's peak, it had a population of some 2,000 people. They kept five sawmills busy supplying lumber for buildings like this residence.

This photo of H.P. Stimler and friends is captioned "Me and the other boys found Goldfield." Later Stimler established the Belmont News Depot, where a variety of Nevada and California papers were available.

Few visitors find their way to Belmont today, but the town has a small population of permanent and part-time residents who look after the historic buildings.

transcontinental railroad, many Chinese workers moved to the mines of California and Nevada. Belmont's Chinese community even boasted its own restaurant at one point. But ethnic friction occasionally appeared. The *Reporter* complained, for example, that Chinese laundry services were becoming expensive. "The Celestials have combined against us and demand six dollars for washing," the editor observed. "A few good washerwomen would do well here."

Conflict between the Cornish and Irish miners who constituted the bulk of the town's labor force went far beyond verbal sparring. The ancient enmity surfaced in Belmont in 1867

when work at the Silver Bend mine was temporarily suspended. Whatever the reason for the shutdown, the Irish miners employed there suspected that the work stoppage had been used to get them to leave town so that they could be replaced by Cornishmen who would work more cheaply. Consequently, on the evening of April 17, R. B. Canfield, general agent for the company, was seized by a mob and ridden through town on a rail. After a stop at the Highbridge saloon, the miners resumed their procession until they were challenged by Louis Bodrow, a former lawman from Austin. A fight broke out between Bodrow and Pat Dignon, one of the mob leaders. This in turn led to a general melee, which left both Irish protesters and Cornish bystanders wounded. When the crowd

Belmont was briefly the seat of Nye County. The courthouse, which is the imposing brick structure at the end of the road, is slowly being renovated.

finally dispersed, both Bodrow and Dignon were dead.

There was another violent episode in May 1874—perhaps involving the two conflicting ethnic groups, perhaps not—but it left three more miners just as dead as Bodrow and Dignon. It began when a couple of Pennsylvania miners, Charlie McIntyre and Jack Walker, got into an argument over cards with one of the local residents, H. H. Sutherland. Walker pulled a gun and wounded Sutherland, while a stray bullet from one of the men hit another local man, Bill Doran, in the leg. The Pennsylvania men were jailed pending

One of Belmont's most impressive buildings is the Highbridge mill seen here. Its bricks were fashioned from high-grade clay found 4 miles from town and fired in local kilns.

131

(Opposite) A close-up of the remains of the Cosmopolitan Hotel. Belmont could draw upon inexpensive local supplies of timber, stone, and brick for construction.

(Left) This plot in the Belmont cemetery holds the remains of a William Anderson, who died in 1886 at the age of 65. He seems to have no fewer than three headstones.

(Below) The ruins of what was once a print shop serve as a reminder that Belmont in its heyday had at least three operating newspapers. Like those of other mining communities, the editors of these publications practiced a colorful brand of journalism.

trial, but one night a mob of Belmont citizens decided to turn the wheels of justice a little faster. Sheriff Jim Caldwell found the prisoners in the morning suspended by their necks from the rafters of the jail. Doran, the local wounded in the gambling fracas, also became a casualty of the affair when he died after the amputation of his leg. The *Courier* lost little time eulogizing the deceased. "He is said to have been a bad man," it reported, "and though it is perhaps inhuman to rejoice over the death of anyone, it was a fortunate occurrence for him, as his untimely death was a certainty, sooner or later."

The Belmont economy suffered a temporary decline in 1868/69 as the local ore veins seemed to be tapering off and newer, more profitable mines were opening in the nearby White Pine District. The gloomy predictions regarding Belmont's demise proved to be premature, however, for new mines opened in 1873 and prosperity returned. Belmont's second boom period lasted until 1887, when the ore finally ran out. Even then the town hung on. Like many other early mining operations, the Belmont stamp mills were crude affairs that reduced their ore inefficiently. In 1907, more advanced mills began reworking the Belmont mine dumps, and they recovered enough silver to stay in business through World War I.

Even in the decades that followed the collapse of the town's mining industry Belmont remained populated to some degree, but the many ruins that surround the few current residents testify to the community's great decline. At its height, Belmont's tree-lined streets gave the town a shaded, relaxed character, while the many stores and shops offered such luxuries as Chicago hams and butter from Iowa. A racetrack on the outskirts of town competed with saloons and sporting houses for the easy money of lonely miners while the school, the church, the theater, and the courthouse gave evidence of more civilized pursuits. The solid ruins of Belmont will remind visitors of the town's former glory for a while yet before the lonely Nevada desert reclaims it all.

(Above) Impoverished Berlin miners, standing on this precipice perhaps, dreamed of Howling Cave, supposedly located across the desolate valley in the distance. Here, deep within Paradise Peak, Indians secreted a trove of gold stolen from whites.

(Opposite) The Nevada desert gave up its wealth to the miners of Berlin only reluctantly, after the application of massive amounts of machinery.

One could say, without much fear of contradiction, that Berlin, Nevada, has the longest history of any ghost town anywhere, for life there can be traced back 180 million years. One of the major tourist attractions is an ichthyosaur fossil site close to the town. History is properly about people, however, not extinct reptiles, and measured on a human scale, the history of Berlin is much briefer. In fact, its human history lasted only about 15 years.

Nye County, Nevada, which encompasses some of the nation's most productive mining districts, has produced consistent quantities of gold, silver, and less valuable metals since the 1860s. Berlin, located on the western slope of the Toiyabe Range, was not among the county's wealthiest strikes. It never competed seriously with richer and longer lasting ore veins at Belmont, Goldfield, and Tonopah, and although one finds 19th-century forecasts of great optimism, Berlin was a relatively short-lived and low-flying meteor in Nevada mining history.

A Nevada politician named Bell was the first to locate a mining claim at Berlin. He extracted some silver from the site in about 1895; but after working it for three years, he

(Right) Thanks to the acquisition of several stamp mills and an influx of additional equipment, the Nevada Mining Company had ample facilities for reducing Berlin's relatively poor silver ore. This overview of the town with a mill on the right was taken circa 1901/02.

(Below) Berlin is maintained in a state of "arrested decay" by the Nevada Division of State Parks, so that the buildings, including the stagecoach station seen here, appear as ruins but are protected from vandalism.

Although Berlin was never very prosperous nor large, it was conveniently located, which made it ideally suited for a stage line to nearby mining communities. The town's stagecoach station is pictured here.

determined that a more substantially capitalized company would be able to exploit the mine better than he, and he sold out to a New York mining entrepreneur named John G. Stokes. Stokes' Nevada Mining Company went into its new venture in a big way. In addition to buying Bell out, it also acquired the Pioneer and Knickerbocker stamp mills near Ione, Nevada. Those investments, plus the additional equipment it brought in, gave Stokes a 30-stamp mill at Berlin for reducing the relatively poor silver ore.

Berlin was never large, but at its peak during the first decade of this century, it boasted a population of 250 people and featured a general store, a post office, an automotive repair shop, and even a stage line to nearby camps like Ione, Union, and Grantsville.

Because its ore was of relatively poor quality, Berlin's economy was always rather shaky; it fluctuated from periods of modest activity to periods of no activity at all as the mines waxed and waned. As in similar western communities, improved technology pumped new life into the Berlin economy by reworking the tailings or waste heaps of ore, to extract the silver or gold that cruder efforts had missed. Although a newspaper in Goldfield, Nevada, estimated that in 1908 enough ore remained in Berlin to keep the mills going for three more years, the operation shut down in 1909. But the tenacious miners refused to be beaten. Between 1911 and 1914, a 50-ton cyanide plant went to work on the tailings and the town struggled on. Finally defeat overtook Berlin, for even with the improved technology, the mill operators could only extract about $2.50 per ton.

Although Berlin was abandoned by the beginning of World War I, the milling machinery remained in place throughout the 1920s and 1930s, as if in hope that some mining genius would devise yet another way of extracting more silver from the tailings. But it was not to be—at least the technology has not been found yet—and the equipment was moved to more profitable digs during World War II.

As miners sweated out every dime they earned and prayed for a new strike in a richer vein, life in Berlin was not entirely grim. Residents of Union, Nevada, only 1¼ miles from Berlin, worked out a simple source of comfort that almost certainly attracted their neighbors. They piped icy water from a mountain stream into a large metal

137

tank, where the sun warmed it to a comfortable temperature during the day. Beneath the tank was an old tub into which one could draw warm water for a soothing evening bath. Lack of privacy seems not to have been a problem in those presumably all-male communities, for the tub was completely unenclosed. The miners of Union and Berlin may not have been the wealthiest in Nevada, but one suspects they were the cleanest.

One of Berlin's nicest attributes for the modern ghost-town aficionado is its commanding location in the foothills above a wide valley. It can be spotted from a good many miles away. On the other side of the valley is Paradise Peak, and one can be certain that many an exhausted Berlin miner sat in front of his cabin at the end of an unprofitable day and contemplated the Indian legend that spoke of treasures in that mountain's belly.

According to the legend, Indians were alarmed during the early days of Nevada mining by the violent effects of greed for gold upon the white men. Whenever the Indians would acquire some of the precious ore through trade or from raids on the whites, they would take it to a cave in Paradise Peak where they believed (thanks to the wind howling through apertures in the walls) a deity resided. They used the gold as an offering to mitigate the white man's violence and bring peace to the region. Berlin miners were acquainted with Indians who claimed to know the location of the cave, but of course they refused to take any whites there because to do so would surely have defeated the purpose of the offerings. Poor as the returns were from the Berlin mines, few, if any, of the men

Nestled in the foothills of western Nevada's Toiyabe Range is Berlin, visible for many miles across the clear desert terrain.

The ore at Berlin, which traveled down chutes like the one seen here, paid only $2.50 per ton at best, barely enough to keep the town alive for 15 years.

who worked there were tempted to abandon them in quest of the Howling Cave.

A great deal of Berlin's charm as a ghost town results from its high state of preservation. It was fortunate in having been well cared for by the mining company even after its abandonment. More recently its preservation has been supervised by the Nevada Division of State Parks, which acquired the site in the 1970s. Responding to the preservationist impulse of the 1960s, which bore fruit in such legislation as the National Historic Preservation Act of 1966, the state became aware of the historic value of such places and of its obligation to protect their integrity. Berlin is currently maintained in what is called "a state of arrested decay." Thus, visitors can appreciate the town's antiquity while being restrained from causing further deterioration or vandalism to its structures.

This photo taken in 1914 shows miners working the tailings, or waste heaps of ore, to extract quantities of silver or gold that cruder efforts had missed. But even improved technology couldn't save Berlin and it was abandoned a few years later.

(Right) At its peak, which came shortly after 1900, Berlin had a population of about 250. All of the town residences were modest structures like this one, owned by a Mrs. Stevens.

(Below) John G. Stokes installed this large stamp mill around the turn of the century for the large-scale processing of Berlin's poor ore.

(Above) Today, mining machinery in remarkably good condition is scattered throughout town, creating an interesting outdoor museum.

141

(Above) Even though a fire destroyed some two-thirds of the town in June 1932, Bodie, California, still contains hundreds of buildings and is administered as a state park.

(Opposite) Law and order were slow to reach this remote community, and many a "badman from Bodie" made the morgue, seen here, almost as profitable to operate as one of the mines.

"A wonderfully refreshing picture of desolation" is how journalist J. Ross Browne described the environs of Bodie, California, when he visited the town in 1865. Bodie's treeless surroundings, well above the timber line at 9,000 feet, no doubt accounted for the "desolation" he observed. What made it "wonderfully refreshing" were the rich veins of gold—then being vigorously worked—and Bodie's many saloons, where, Browne says, a "fine spring of water, aided by a little snake-medicine, set us all right."

According to legend, Bodie owed its discovery to a wounded rabbit and its name to a signpainter's mistake. In 1858 or 1859, a prospector named Waterman S. ("Bill") Body, passing through the area, shot a rabbit, and in trying to dig it out of its hole discovered gold. Body was was not able to exploit his discovery, though, for he froze to death in the snow that winter. His three companions were unable even to find the corpse until the following spring. Body's bad luck continued even in death. First his name was misspelled when the town was founded about 1860. Some blame an illiterate signpainter, but others claim the change was deliberate to ensure the correct pronunciation of the name. Then in 1879, long after the town bearing Body's misspelled name had been established and fortunes were being made in the gold he had discovered, some citizens decided that his bones had lain in an unmarked grave long enough. So they exhumed his remains and placed them in the new town cemetery, intending to erect a monument over them. But by the time they got around to it, President James A. Garfield had been assassinated, and patriotic Bodieans appropriated funds for a monument to the nation's chief executive instead of to their town's founder.

Bodie got off to a slow start. Although the Bodie Mining District had been formed on July 10, 1860, the much richer veins in nearby Aurora, Nevada, attracted many more miners than did the California town. In 1864, Bodie consisted of fewer than 20 frame buildings. But, after the Comstock Lode began to dwindle in the late 1870s, miners came to Bodie in increasing numbers and in a couple of fortunate accidents discovered richer veins than anyone had previously thought existed.

One of those lucky breaks came in the mid-1870s when a cave-in at the Standard mine exposed a much richer pocket of ore than that which the miners had been working. The two men who had bought it for $950 sold out for $65,000 after extracting some $37,000 in gold. In the nearby Bodie mine, laborers struck a very rich vein and kept the news from the owners until they could change their wages to shares of stock. Thereafter, interests in the mine, which had been selling at 25 cents per share, rose to $55. Miners began earning almost $900 per day.

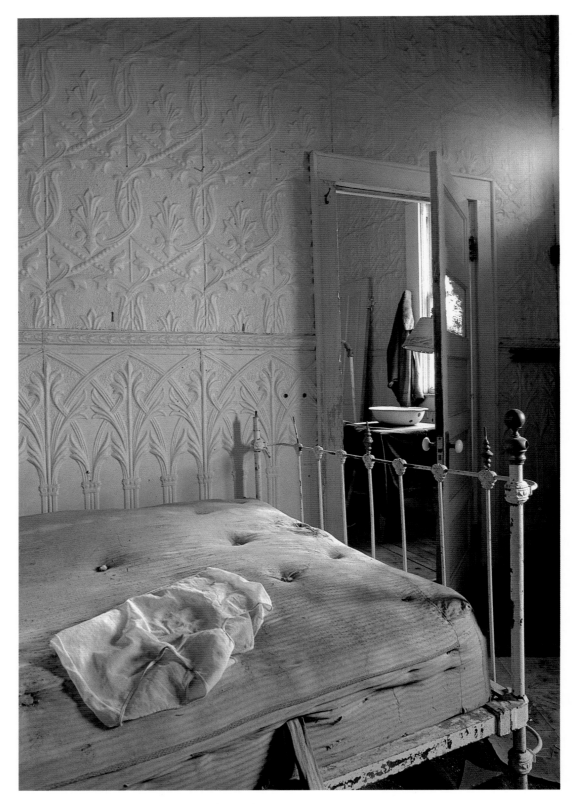

As this bedroom in the Bodie Hotel reveals, some of the town's buildings are furnished with authentic 19th- and early-20th-century items, but most are opened only for special groups with reservations.

(Opposite) The Swazel Hotel on Main Street. The grassy thoroughfares and the heavy patina of the wooden buildings give Bodie a true ghost-town feeling.

The Conway House, one of Bodie's hotels, is in the foreground of this photo, and the Standard mine is in the distance. In the 1870s, the Standard was the site of a lucky cave-in that revealed one of the town's richest gold veins.

Bodie reached its pinnacle in the late 1870s, when it had perhaps as many as 20,000 residents living along Main Street, "like an elongated banana on a cord," as one elegant observer put it. Its business establishments included 60 saloons (more, the *Reno Weekly Gazette* speculated, than one could find along any street of similar length anywhere in the world), numerous gambling halls, some breweries, and no fewer than five newspapers—a record for literary output that few western cities of any size could equal at that time. At the other end of the cultural scale, a substantial population of ladies-of-the-night plied their ancient trade in Bodie. Along a street known as Virgin Alley, such characters as Big Bonanza, Beautiful Doll, and Big Nell ministered to lonely miners' needs.

Prostitution was not the most pressing social problem during Bodie's heyday, for law and order were slow in reaching that remote community. Bodie was, in fact, renowned for the violent nature of its citizens. To be a "badman from Bodie"—as a common phrase of the day had it—meant that you were a rough character indeed.

Claim-jumping, of course, was the most common cause of conflict. When such a dispute broke out in August 1879 between the owners of the Owyhee and Jupiter mines, both sides hired professional gunmen to advance their claims and civil war reigned for

several days. Eventually the members of the Bodie Miners Union took up arms as a vigilante militia to stop the fighting. Then a vigilante court settled the dispute, ruling against the Jupiter men and ordering the firm's superintendent and five of his subordinates to leave town within 24 hours.

The settlement of the Owyhee–Jupiter conflict did not bring peace to the community, for vigilante justice could be just as ruthless as the force utilized by claim-jumpers. For some time greedy, violent men used the power of the gun in Bodie to gain whatever they could. Shootings became almost daily events and usually went unpunished. But, in 1879, when one man was shot by an outraged husband for dancing with his wife on New Year's Eve, a mob lynched the killer publicly in a desperate attempt to assert a kind of community order. The hanging produced something of the desired effect within the confines of the town itself, but the gunmen who had been robbing Bodie citizens and jumping claims merely moved outside of town. There they turned their attention to shipments of gold passing through the narrow canyon between Bodie and Aurora. Wells Fargo Company assigned more guards to the shipments, but with only limited improvement in security.

Violence in Bodie declined only with the decline of the town itself. By

During the early years of the 20th century, long after Bodie's boom days were behind it, the town still boasted a baseball team. Its members posed for this group portrait on July 6, 1909.

No town ever had a better booster than Bodie's banker, Jim Cain, seen here on the day of his marriage to Martha D. Wells, September 17, 1879. For many years after Bodie's demise, Cain continued to open his bank each day, awaiting business that never came.

1883, when gold production began to decrease, it became clear that the celebrated community's best days were behind it. Nevertheless, many miners hung on, and in fact Bodie's most significant urban improvement—the installation of electric lights—came in 1893. Some mines continued to produce until 1955.

By far the most optimistic of Bodie's citizens was banker Jim Cain. For many years after Bodie's demise, he continued to open his bank each day, awaiting business that never came. Finally, even Cain had to acknowledge the futility of finding banking prospects among the occasional sheepherders and prospectors who wandered through Bodie in the course of their lonely occupations. He moved his enterprise to Bridgeport, Nevada.

A fire in June 1932 destroyed roughly two-thirds of Bodie, tragically eroding its status as one of California's largest and best-preserved ghost towns. Nevertheless, the buildings that remain have weathered beautifully in the pure mountain air, the patina of their wood shining in the sun with little evidence of rot and decay.

148

(*Opposite, top*) Main Street was home to an estimated 20,000 residents in the late 1870s. Life on this street was "like an elongated banana on a cord," according to one contemporary observer.

(*Opposite, bottom*) Sam Leon's Bar. There were no fewer than 60 saloons on Main Street in the late 1870s. A Reno newspaper considered this to be a record for a town of Bodie's size.

(*Right*) Bodie's one-room school testifies to the community's civilized aspirations, a happy contrast with its more pervasive reputation for violence and lawlessness.

(*Below*) This sawmill on Park Street provided both lumber and firewood.

(Above) In the 1840s, Hornitos was a small Mexican town, but the Gold Rush of 1849 brought hordes of Italian, Chinese, and Anglo miners to the area.

(Opposite) The interior of the Catholic church, looking toward the altar. This church, which still serves Hornitos' small population of farmers, is one of the town's best-preserved historic buildings.

When the 1840s began, Hornitos was a typical sleepy Mexican town. By the end of the decade, however, it had been hit by such a succession of political, economic, and social bombshells that its character had changed completely. The Mexican War, for one thing, resulted in the United States' annexation of Hornitos along with the rest of California in 1848; by 1850 the territory had become a state. For another thing, the discovery of gold 100 miles to the north brought a wave of miners to Hornitos in 1849. These fortune seekers were an ethnically diverse group. Thus, Anglos, Italians, and Chinese vied with the Hispanics for places in the diggings. Finally, the town experienced a crime wave, as famous outlaws seeking a shortcut to wealth were attracted by the rich, gold-laden quartz deposits.

Located in what is now Mariposa County on the western slope of the Sierra Nevada Mountains, Hornitos was almost at the extreme southern end of what was called the "Mother Lode," a belt of gold deposits some 120 miles long. At an average elevation of 2,500 feet and varying from a few hundred feet to a couple of miles in width, these deposits were thought of by early miners as the source, or "mother," of the placers—pockets of gold in stream beds—that they had been mining at lower elevations. Mining the placers had been relatively easy and profitable even with the most primitive equipment: one man with a pan or a small team with a sluice box could wash large quantities of gold from the gravel and mud in which it lay. At the higher elevations of the Mother Lode, though, the gold was solidly embedded in quartz deposits from which it could only be extricated by means of hard labor and expensive equipment. One positive factor in regard to the quartz deposits near Hornitos was the ready supply of laborers, but even they proved to be too few for the needs of the mine's operators, and others were imported in large numbers.

The variety of structures in the town reflected the ethnic diversity of those who came to work in the mines. *Hornitos* is a Spanish word for outdoor brick ovens, but the name in this case derived from the graves shaped like those ovens that had once filled the cemetery around the community's small Catholic church. When the Chinese arrived in the early 1850s, laundries and opium dens made their appearance. Commercially minded Anglos and Italians built stores and saloons to meet the miners' needs, and Hornitos took on a cosmopolitan look.

One of the more curious structures was the jail. Calling to mind a medieval dungeon, it featured a large iron ring in the floor of the holding cell, to which inmates could be chained while awaiting trial, thus pro-

viding an added measure of security to the adobe structure. Another oddity was the large tunnel of adobe bricks that ran beneath one side of the main street to the basement of the saloon on the other. Historians of a romantic bent claim that it was built by the Hispanic citizens for Joaquin Murietta, a Robin Hood–like outlaw with a price on his head. Murietta liked to drink in the saloon and the tunnel would have given him a means of escape had he

(Opposite) **The interior of this jailhouse resembles a medieval dungeon, with a large iron ring embedded in the floor, to which prisoners could be chained.**

(Below) **C. B. Cavagnaro, whose general store is pictured here, was one of a number of Italian-American merchants drawn to Hornitos by the town's large ethnic population.**

been trapped there. A more mundane explanation is that it was a way to get beer from the brewery on the other side of the street to the saloon's storage area. Perhaps it served both purposes.

Murietta was one of the town's most colorful residents. His career is clouded in romantic legend and insufficient records, but the murders he committed are at its hard historical core and they contain important truths regarding the social tensions of the Mother Lode country in the 1850s. Those tensions were rooted in two developments: first, declining production as the easy gold of the earlier years gave way to the realities of hard-rock mining; and, second, the pressure the older Hispanic residents felt, on the one hand, from

frugal Chinese laborers who would work for almost nothing and, on the other hand, from the Anglo mining entrepreneurs who made great fortunes but wanted to pay their laborers as little as possible. Murietta and his partner, Three-Fingered Jack, took it upon themselves to avenge their people, the poor Hispanics, by exterminating the Chinese and robbing the Anglos.

The Chinese suffered the outlaw's attacks without being able to respond, but the Anglos retaliated in 1853 by offering a $6,000 reward for the head of Joaquin Murietta to Harry Love. Love was a captain of the California Rangers with an unsavory reputation almost equal to that of Murietta himself. He and his men caught up with Murietta and Three-Fingered Jack on July 25 and killed both of the outlaws. Muri-

etta's head and Jack's mutilated hand were preserved in whiskey until they reached Stockton, where they were placed in medical alcohol. Though there was some question about the actual identities of the murdered men, their remains became a popular attraction throughout the Mother Lode country for many years, and thousands paid a dollar apiece to get a look at them.

Joaquin Murietta was not the only famous person in Hornitos history. Gen. Ulysses S. Grant once stayed in the Hornitos hotel. No mining expert, the Civil War hero had nevertheless been brought to California by a mining entrepreneur to inspect and give his

(Opposite) Hornitos' Hispanic heritage is conspicuous in the adobe construction of many of its older buildings.

(Right) This cow skull is a reminder of Hornitos' livestock-based economy before and after the short-lived—but colorful—gold rush era.

(Below) Wagons like this one transported millions of dollars in gold ore from California's Mother Lode country during the gold rush. Hornitos is at the southern end of the Mother Lode.

approval to a dubious enterprise that the entrepreneur hoped to unload at a high price.

Not all business ventures in Hornitos were dubious. D. Ghirardelli, an enterprising Italian businessman, began his chocolate manufacturing business, of all things, in Hornitos. The ruins of the building were once marked by a bronze plaque. Perhaps Ghirardelli learned, as one might suspect, that miners' tastes ran more to alcohol than chocolate, for he soon moved to San Francisco to build his candy empire.

Finally, John C. Frémont, the famous explorer whose role in the Bear Flag Revolt against the Mexican government in California was either infamous or instrumental, depending on one's point of view, was not exactly a Hornitos resident, but his huge Mariposa estate was a very close neighbor. One of the complicated episodes in his complicated career concerned the boundaries of this Mariposa estate, which had not been surveyed and was only vaguely described at the time that he acquired title to it. When gold was discovered in the Mother Lode country, Frémont shifted the borders of his holdings some 50 miles to the east before having them surveyed, in order to include some of the richest gold

John C. Frémont had a huge estate near Hornitos, and when gold was discovered in the Mother Lode country, he managed to incorporate some of the richest veins into his holdings. The townsite itself only escaped the "Pathfinder's" land grab by a few miles.

(Below) Although he was no mining expert, Gen. Ulysses S. Grant (fifth from the right) was brought to California by a mining entrepreneur to inspect and give his approval to a dubious get-rich-quick scheme. Mrs. Grant is to her husband's right and the Civil War hero's son, Ulysses S. Grant, Jr., is next to her.

The Catholic church and graveyard dominate
a distant view of Hornitos.

veins. The townsite of Hornitos only escaped the Frémont land grab by a few miles.

The town of Hornitos did not survive the gold rush. When the mines played out, the miners left, and even the herdsmen who had preceded the gold rush seemed little inclined to stick around. During the present century, a different breed of entrepreneur learned that Mariposa County's most enduring gold was to be found on grapevines instead of in quartz deposits, and Mariposa County wines are among California's most celebrated vintages. But the wine industry has not revitalized the town of Hornitos. Its church, Joaquin Murietta's tunnel, and a few ruined buildings remain unused and largely unvisited.

Joaquin Murietta, a Robin Hood–like outlaw (left), and his partner, Three-Fingered Jack, preyed upon the Chinese and Anglo residents of Hornitos in retaliation for what they saw as the exploitation of the local Hispanics.

Aqui descansan los restos mortales de Esquipula Moreno y sus dos Hijas, Manuelita de 9 Años, y Lolita Moreno, que Murio, el 14 de Diciembre de 1880 Edad 18 Años.

(Above) Hornito is a Spanish term for a type of outdoor oven which resembles some of the graves in this cemetery.

(Opposite) The remains of the D. Ghirardelli store remind visitors that the celebrated San Francisco chocolate magnate got his start in this small mining town.

PHOTO CREDITS

All of the color photographs in this volume are courtesy of Lynn Radeka. The historic photographs were supplied by the following sources:

California Department of Parks and Recreation, Audio-Visual Collection 147, 148

California State Library 156, 158

Center for Southwest Research, General Library, University of New Mexico, 97 (bottom) (neg. no. 000-179-06360, Henry A. Schmidt, Photographer), 101 (neg. no 000-179-0717, Henry A. Schmidt, photographer)

Central Nevada Historical Society 123, 136

Colorado Historical Society 13, 15, 22, 25, 28

Denver Public Library, Western History Department 33

Idaho State Historical Society 75 (Photo #77-19.20), 77 (Photo #77-19.1)

Jerome Historical Society 116

Library of Congress 97 (top)

Mary Louise Loe 81

Montana Historical Society 55, 58, 62, 68

Museum of New Mexico 91, 93, 107,

Nevada Historical Society 129, 140

Wyoming State Museum 39, 40, 41, 47

ACKNOWLEDGEMENTS

The producers of *Ghost Towns of the Old West* gratefully acknowledge the following individuals who assisted in the creation of this book:

Belmont, Nevada, Paula Kniefel; Bodie State Park, Mark Pupich; Bureau of Land Management, Missoula, Montana, Chuck Hollenbaugh; Cabezon, New Mexico, Mr. and Mrs. Benny Lucero; California State Library, Kathleen Eustis; California Department of Parks and Recreation, Interpretive Services Department, Donna Pozzi; Center for Southwest Research, University of New Mexico, Stella deSaRego; Central Nevada Historical Society, William Metscher; Colorado Historical Society, Rebecca Lintz; Denver Public Library, Western History Department, Kathey Swan; Garnet, Montana, Dwight Gappert; Gold Hill, Nevada, Herb Robbins; Idaho State Historical Society, Elizabeth Jacox; Jerome Historical Society, Nancy Smith; Molson, Washington, Mary Louise Loe; Montana Historical Society, Bonnie Morgan; Nevada Historical Society, Erik Lauritzen; Museum of New Mexico, Arthur Olivas; Shakespeare Ghost Town, Janaloo Hill Hough, Manny Hough; South Pass City, Wyoming, Todd Gunther; University of Nevada, David P. Robrock; Wyoming State Museum, LaVaughn Bresnahan.

Shakespeare, New Mexico